www.CaminoGuide.net

CAMINO DE SANTIAGO
Practical Preparation and Background

**AN OUTLINE OF ITS HISTORY AND CULTURE
AND A CAMINO PHRASEBOOK**

Second Edition
updated February 2016

Gerald Kelly
Copyright 2016

INTRODUCTION

I remember the first time I heard of the Camino...

My then girlfriend and I had driven down in blazing sunshine from her house on the river Lot only to find the Basque coast, as it often is, shrouded in misty rain. We then spent the entire weekend bickering.

On the Sunday afternoon, in Jean Pied de Port, we stood on a bridge over the river Nive and looked at each other and laughed for the first time that day. Because both of us knew we were thinking about shoving the other in. It was shortly afterwards we saw some people in hiking gear with backpacks and she told me, 'People still walk from here to Galicia, it's an old pilgrimage route.' I don't remember my exact reaction but it was something along the lines of:

Why the hell would anybody want to do that?

Ten years later I still haven't found a simple answer to that question. But, I've had a lot of fun looking! Because, despite my initial cynicism, the seed of an idea planted in me that day has grown to be something of an obsession. This book is the product of that obsession. I hope you'll find it informative and helpful and that it will see you safely to your earthly destination.

Gerald Kelly

What is the Camino?

The Camino de Santiago, or the Way of St James, is a medieval pilgrimage route which brought pilgrims from all corners of Europe, across Spain to the city of Santiago de Compostela, believed by many to be the final resting place of Saint James (the Greater) the Apostle.

It's existed for about a thousand years, and all through those centuries thousands of people each year have set out from their homes to travel to Santiago on foot or on horseback. It was one of many pilgrimage routes in Europe but for many centuries it was the most popular.

In the last thirty years the Camino Francés, or French Way, from southern France to Santiago, has become very popular with walkers. It is now traversed by thousands of people every year, for a wide variety of reasons. It takes about 30 days to walk.

Other routes such as the Vía de la Plata, from Seville, and the Camino del Norte, along the north coast of Spain, have also become more popular, but not to the same degree as the Camino Francés.

About this book

This book is intended for people planning to walk the Camino for the first time. It contains detailed, practical, impartial information and advice to help you prepare for your Camino. It is based on the author's personal experience and on the experiences of many other pilgrims.

Rather than trying to reduce Camino preparation to a check-list, by telling you to do A, B and C, it is there to assist you in making informed decisions and help you avoid pitfalls. It covers (among others) the following areas:

- **Money:** How much walking the Camino costs
- **Travel:** How to get to your starting point
- **Physical preparation:** Getting to the required level of fitness
- **Packing:** Equipment you need and what you don't need
- **Which section and when:** When to walk, where to walk
- **What to expect:** The Camino experience

In addition, there's an introduction to both **Spanish** and **Camino history**, a **Spanish phrasebook** with vocabulary chosen to cover Camino necessities, and background information of all sorts to help you plan and prepare.

This book is a companion to the books *Walking Guide to the Camino de Santiago* and *Walking Guide to the Vía de la Plata* (also available from Amazon in Kindle and printed formats), which contain the information you'll need about accommodation and services, etc. while walking the Camino Francés and the Vía de la Plata. However, since this book is all about preparation, it can be used entirely independently of any walking guide.

Although much of the information in this book could be useful for any Camino, some parts of it refer specifically to the Camino Francés.

This is a self-published book. Please accept my apologies for any mistakes. You can help by sending corrections and any comments about content or omissions to *info@caminoguide.net*. Because a new copy of the book is printed every time somebody orders one, corrections and additions can be made immediately, without having to wait for a new edition.

The 2013 edition of this book is the product of several years learning and reflection, and three new Camino adventures since the first edition. It's an attempt to rectify the shortcomings of the first edition, based on the feedback from readers. The entire book has been revised, and many parts of it have been rewritten and extended.

This edition, published in January 2014, has been professionally proofread.

MEASUREMENT UNITS AND EURO AMOUNTS

All distances are given in the **metric system** (kilometres and metres) and all times are given in the **24 hour clock** (09:00 = 9am, 18:00 = 6pm).

Temperatures are given in Celsius. Celsius temperatures are easy:

0°C = freezing point of water, 10°C = cold, 20°C = warm
30°C = hot, 100°C = boiling point of water

There's a handy converter here *www.celsius-to-fahrenheit.com*

The format for writing **amounts** reflects the most commonly used format in Spain. eg. One euro = 1€, fifty cents = 0,50€, one thousand euros = 1.000€ (see page 58).

A NOTE ON THE WORD *PILGRIM*

As I'm not particularly religious in any conventional sense, it took me years before I came to see myself as a pilgrim, and to use that word unselfconsciously. Now, I call myself a pilgrim when I go on the Camino, and I regard all of the other people there as pilgrims too. I no longer see this word as being uniquely associated with organised religion, and I use it inclusively in this guide to refer to everybody who sets out from their home on the open road looking for something (meaning, answers, solace, purpose, etc.)

THANKS / BUÍOCHAS / GRACIAS / DANKE

Roisín Cuddihy, Dalan de Bri, Ana Belén Molina, Sofía Montes de la Riva, Philip ó Ceallaigh, Robbie Turner, Dr Hans Weber. Everybody who's contributed to *www.CaminoGuide.net* and to this book.

References to the Glossary

Wherever you see (G) after a word it means there's an explanatory note about it in the Glossary on page 136.

PLANNING AND PREPARATION

Everybody prepares in their own way, everybody packs in their own way and everybody walks the Camino in their own way. The following are suggestions to help you prioritise.

Physical preparation

If you're unsure about your physical preparedness, try walking your target daily distance with a full backpack.

If you struggle, you need to either set yourself an exercise regime and work your way up to your target. Alternatively, you could reduce your daily distance target for the first week or so until your fitness level improves. Accommodation is plentiful on the Camino and it can be taken at an extremely leisurely pace if you so desire. The key is finding a pace that suits you.

Walking long distances every day is different from doing it occasionally because your body doesn't get a chance to recover and heal. It takes about a week to find your rhythm, so set yourself modest goals for the first few days.

If you've never before walked long distances, it's important to get an idea before you set out of what it feels like and what you're capable of. Finding and sticking to your own pace is very important in avoiding injury.

Your physical preparation should be done while breaking in your walking footwear and getting accustomed to carrying your backpack at its packed weight. It doesn't matter what you put in it - it can be water in plastic bottles (1 litre of water = 1kg) - as long as it weights 7kg or 8kg minimum. You should aim to do your Camino training from as early as possible in "full Camino mode": Backpack, boots, everything.

You should begin well before you're due to leave. Try doing three or four short (one or two hour) hikes a week and one longer one (always carrying your backpack). The longer one could start off being two or three hours but you should work this up gradually to about five hours (about 20km). Include a few hills. If you can manage that you'll be fine. You don't need to be super fit to walk the Camino, the chances are many people reading this are fit enough already.

Which part to walk?

Walking the entire Camino Francés from Saint-Jean to Santiago (775km) takes about 31 days at 25km a day. If you haven't got 31 days to spare, below are some suggestions for shorter itineraries.

If you've got limited time: The most obvious suggestion would be to walk the last **111km from Sarria**. If getting a Compostela certificate (G) is important to you, then that's what you should do. If you start in Sarria it's important that you get at least one other stamp (see under *Credencial*, page 38), besides the one from the hostel where you slept, each day from a hostel or some other establishment along the route. This is to provide extra proof when you go to the Pilgrims' Office in Santiago that you did actually walk it.

On the other hand, if you're more interested in experiencing the Camino with the intention of one day walking the whole thing, bear in mind that the Sarria to Santiago stretch can become very crowded in summer. Some pilgrims, having walked many kilometres, find these last few days tough just because there are so many people. So, if you want to experience a little of the history, solitude, camaraderie and beauty of the Camino, consider trying one of the following:

Saint-Jean to Puente la Reina is about five days walking, or six if you break the stage from Saint-Jean to Roncesvalles. It takes in some beautiful and historical villages, the city of Pamplona and some lovely scenery. Alternatively starting in Roncesvalles will avoid that difficult first stage and allow you to finish in Estella.

Pamplona to Logroño is about four days with two more to **Santo Domingo de la Calzada**. Again, beautiful, historic and the city of Logroño is fantastic. Both cities are easily accessible by bus and train.

If you want to experience something of the **Meseta** (G), you could start in **Burgos** and walk about four days to **Carrión de los Condes** or about ten days to **León**. The Meseta gets a bad press because there isn't much pretty scenery, but some people consider this flat bit in the middle to be the high point of their experience. On the Meseta, the very lack of things to see is, in itself, something to see.

If you've got about two weeks you could consider starting in **León or Astorga** and walking to Santiago. Or you could stop in Sarria, which would be about eight or nine days from León.

Of course, the ideal is to walk the whole thing in one go. It takes about a month and it has a strange symmetry. Up to Pamplona you're still a child learning how things work, and wide-eyed at everything you see around you. Then to Burgos you're an adolescent, excitable and curious. Then the middle part as far as Astorga is the part of the Camino, that's like the long, sunny afternoon of life that you think will never end. Then gradually the mountains drift into view for several days before you reach them and you relish the thought of climbing them because you're an experienced walker and as fit as a fiddle but you're also a bit settled in your ways; you have your 'Camino family' and you feel like you've known them for ever. There's also the feeling that you're slowly drifting towards an end point. Which, when you reach it is the greatest celebration and outpouring of relief and happiness. Finally, rest!

Finisterre is the bonus, the icing on the cake. An opportunity to reflect on all that has gone before and how it's possible to fit a lifetime's experience into thirty days. And to figure out how the hell you're going to go back to real life.

When to walk?

Most of the Camino is walkable at all times of the year. However, mountainous areas may be difficult or impassible if there is snow and you should follow local advice about how to proceed.

MARCH - APRIL - MAY
Advantages: Good chance of warm, dry weather. Unlikely to find hostels full.
Disadvantages: Possibility of rain, especially in the west.

JUNE - JULY - AUGUST
Advantages: Fine weather. Lots of people walking with a good mix of ages and types. All facilities open.
Disadvantages: Can be very hot. Possible problems finding accommodation, especially in the west. Overcrowding on the last 100km.

SEPTEMBER - OCTOBER
Advantages: Like spring, with added advantage of lots of berries and figs to eat.
Disadvantages: Possibility of rain, especially in the west.

NOVEMBER - DECEMBER - JANUARY - FEBRUARY
Advantages: Very few other pilgrims. Cool weather is good for walking.
Disadvantages: Very few other pilgrims. Many hostels and cafés closed. Rain, wind, snow, cold. Short days. Mud.

On the question of overcrowding at peak times, bear in mind that people tend to start their walk at a weekend from one of the major departure points (See Starting Points under Statistics, page 85), with a wave of people leaving Saint-Jean on Saturday and Sunday and passing through Pamplona three days later on Tuesday and Wednesday. This can make a pronounced difference to the numbers walking for four or five days after the major starting points. There is also a bigger wave (a tsunami, if you like) of people who absolutely want to arrive in Santiago amid hordes of people for the feast of St James (25 July). They'll be leaving Saint-Jean around 25 June, and working their way along the Camino during the month of July.

It's also important to emphasise that overcrowding is a problem on the Camino in Galicia, during Holy Week and during July and August. Outside of Galicia and those times you're unlikely to encounter any problems.

Continental (or Peninsular) Spain is in the Central European Time (CET) time-zone (as are France, Germany, Italy, etc.), which in winter is UTC/GMT + 1. In summer this goes forward an hour to become UTC/GMT + 2. But because most of Spain, and all the Camino Francés, is west of the Greenwich Meridian, the sun is at its highest in summer around 14:00. So the hottest part of the day may be later than what you would expect in countries whose time-zone corresponds more closely to solar time.

Walking in winter

Apart from the weather, walking in winter (December, January, February and March) presents other difficulties. Firstly, many **pilgrim hostels** will be closed (sometimes even those that claim to be open all year). This applies especially to small hostels and private hostels. Also many other businesses along the Camino that cater to pilgrims, such as **shops** and **cafés**, shut during winter months or operate with reduced hours.

So, walking in winter requires more planning than walking in summer. However, if you plan your stages to end in or close to a larger town or village (generally, those with several pilgrim hostels) you should always find at least one hostel and other facilities open. Failing that, as a last resort, there's always at least one enterprising individual to fill the gap with alternative accommodation. If you're stuck, try asking local people or in shops and cafés.

It's also a good idea to stock up on basic food (bread, cheese, etc.) when you get the chance, rather than assume you'll be able to do so later in the day. If a village shop is closed, ask around nearby. The chances are you'll be able to find out at what time they will open.

Hospitaleros can often provide you with reliable information about what's open on the next stage. Remember the Spanish for *open/closed* – *abierto/cerrado*. There is also a really useful and regularly updated internet list of winter hostels, it's at *www.aprinca.com/alberguesinvierno*

Packing: What to bring?

One of the great things about the Camino is that you really need very little stuff to do it. This makes it a good exercise in de-cluttering or seeing what's important and what isn't. The two lists below, covering Essential and Inessential Equipment.

Essential equipment: these are the things you **will need** on the Camino. This list doesn't vary much from person to person. The main difference is between summer walking and the rest of the year. eg. You need rainwear all year round but the rainwear you need in August is not the same rainwear you need in January.

Other equipment: The items on this list may be very useful or even essential, under certain circumstances, but you could either buy or find them easily on the Camino. Whether you pack these items depends on the likelihood of needing them, difficulty of buying or finding them, and their weight/bulkiness.

As a general rule, you should aim to carry **no more than 10% of your body weight** in your backpack. So, if you weigh 70kg, you should have no more than 7kg on your back. This suggested maximum assumes you're fairly close to your medically recommended weight. If you're unfit or overweight, you should aim for less than 10%. If your pack is too heavy, you will have difficulties. Find out if your pack is too heavy by carrying a test pack for a test Camino day (at least five or six hours walking).

The Camino is not a wilderness walk and you'll never be more than a couple of hours from a shop or café. However, when packing you should take into account that you will need to carry some food and water. A litre of water weighs 1kg, so at the start of each day you'll have an extra 2kg, or thereabouts, in your backpack.

The **Golden Rule of Packing**: Look at each item and ask **Will I really NEED this to walk the Camino?** If the answer is **no** then leave it at home. If the answer is **maybe,** then think hard about the pros and cons of bringing it.

The number one mistake first-timers make is bringing too much stuff. They nearly kill themselves for the first few days trying to carry it, then have to go to the trouble and expense of sending things home or onwards to Santiago.

If you haven't done this kind of thing before, you should test pack to make sure it all fits and that you can carry it comfortably for eight or so hours (and there is only one way to find out!). Pack heavy items at the bottom of your backpack and close to your body, to get as much weight as possible on your hips rather than on your shoulders. Finding the best adjustment for your backpack is often a matter of trial and error, and what works for one person won't necessarily work for another. Modern backpacks can be adjusted in several ways; experiment with these to find what works best for you. Once on the Camino, you can ask advice from more experienced pilgrims if your backpack feels uncomfortable, or if you're getting shoulder or back pains.

NB. This book does not endorse any particular brands. Many companies produce good equipment and / or clothes, and when one is mentioned here, it's just as an example of what many pilgrims find useful.

The website **caminoguide.net/packing** *goes into more detail about my own personal experience, with links to information about, and photos of, equipment I use personally or which have been recommended by others.*

Packing: Essential equipment

FOOTWEAR

Most pilgrims on the Camino de Santiago bring two pairs of footwear; one for **walking** and one for **resting**. Resting your feet when the day's walk is over is very important and changing to light, comfortable footwear is a good way to do this. This is discussed in more detail below.

Your walking footwear is your single most important piece of equipment. Choosing suitable and comfortable walking footwear, and taking the time to break them in, is very important (See Blisters page 64). If at all possible buy your footwear from a shop that specialises in hiking equipment. A serious outdoor shop will have staff who hike themselves, who'll be able to point you in the direction of the type of footwear you need and who'll know how to measure your feet and match that to a size and type of boot. Consider buying a little bigger than your normal size because your feet will most likely swell after a few weeks walking.

Afternoon or evening is the best time to try on footwear because your feet swell as the day goes on. Wear the socks you intend to wear on the Camino. Make sure you have some wiggle-room for your toes, the should not be jammed together or rubbing of the inside of the shoe.

On the Camino there's quite a lot of walking on gravel paths and paved surfaces so whatever footwear you chose it needs to have good cushioning in the sole.

There are two main options for walking footwear:
   running shoes / trainers or hiking boots.

RUNNING SHOES / TRAINERS

In summer it's possible to walk the Camino in a pair of light running shoes with a thick or cushioned sole.

The **advantage** is that they're light. They're made of soft material so are less likely to cause blisters. They're comfortable to wear in hot weather. They're designed for running on hard surfaces so they give your feet enough support and protection to deal with the distances and terrain involved in walking the Camino. They also usually have a degree of breathability. Unlike boots, running shoes generally need zero cleaning and polishing. Unlike leather boots, running shoes don't need breaking in. They should be comfortable from the beginning, provided you get a pair that suits you and that fits correctly.

The **disadvantages** are that most running shoes aren't waterproof so if it rains (and it always rains at some stage) your feet will get wet. Since it's unlikely to be cold (we're talking about the summer here) or to rain for days at a time, you're not in danger of getting hypothermia and your running shoes should dry out pretty quickly once the sun comes out again. So, wet feet is more an inconvenience than a serious problem.

Another disadvantage in wet weather is that running shoes aren't very good in the mud and they and your socks will quickly be covered in the stuff. This again is more an (unsightly) inconvenience than a major problem, and if you wash your shoes and leave them out to dry, they'll be ready to use again in the morning (although they're unlikely to dry properly until the sun comes out). In addition, shoes don't give as much support and protection to your ankles as full hiking boots. This may lead to fatigue or injury. In summary, running shoes are comfortable and light and great in dry and hot weather, but in wet weather they don't give much protection against the wet or mud.

HIKING BOOTS

Hiking boots are by far the the most popular type of walking footwear among long-distance pilgrims year round and almost the only kind worn outside the summer months. Most pilgrims go for light leather and Gore-Tex mix hiking boots rather than heavier mountaineering type boots.

Their **advantages** are that they are designed for walking long distances over mixed terrain and in variable weather conditions. The high ankle offers some extra support to your ankle and some protection from twists, although this will vary by boot and how tightly you lace them. Most of the light hiking boots people walk the Camino in don't actually offer that much ankle protection, especially if you don't lace them up tightly, as most people don't. (This could be important for inexperienced hikers who may need time before they build strength in their lower legs.) They have a strong, cushioned sole with good all-weather grip. A Gore-Tex layer adds waterproofing and breathability. They offer good protection against the cold when walking in cold weather or on frozen ground. In snow they offer good protection against both the cold and melted snow wetting your feet. An additional benefit, when you're walking in shorts you'll get fewer pebbles in your boots than you will in shoes and you can reduce this again by rolling the tops of your socks over the tops of your boots.

The **disadvantages** of hiking boots include that they're heavier than running shoes and less comfortable in hot weather. They can be quite stiff, if not fully broken in, which increases the danger of blisters. It takes longer to put them on and take them off when you stop for a rest or when you get a pebble in them. Boots are also bulky and so difficult to pack away if you don't want to wear them for your whole walking day. Caring for boots properly is not easy on the Camino (although this may not be an important consideration for you). If they are not properly cared for they will quickly lose their waterproof qualities. The type of care varies by brand of boot so the manufacturer's instructions are the last word on this, but generally it consists of cleaning the boots regularly and treating them with a spray or cream which renews their waterproof qualities and breathability, and lubricates the leather, hence lessening its tendency to crack at bend points. In the context of hiking for 30 or so consecutive days you should ideally be cleaning and treating them every three or four days in order to get the longest possible useful life from them. That would mean bringing an adequate supply of cleaning material with you, adding weight to your pack, which for most people isn't an option. Olive oil, which is available in most Spanish restaurants, is quite good as a leather lubricant, but naturally the manufacturer's recommendations are best. Don't leave wet leather to dry near a heat source; this can damage the leather and lessen its waterproofing.

RESTING FOOTWEAR

The term **resting footwear** refers to the footwear you'll wear when you're finished walking for the day and are going around looking at the sights, or just relaxing. Good resting footwear should be light, because you have to carry it all day. It should be compact enough to fit in your backpack or attachable to your backpack in some way. It should be loose fitting and/or soft so that if you do get blisters or discomfort of any sort your resting footwear won't make them worse. It should be comfortable enough to walk around in and be well ventilated to allow your feet to breathe (and possibly heal) after a long day being cooped up. Other desirable characteristics are that it can be worn in the shower and dries quickly. It's also potentially very useful if your resting footwear is capable of replacing your main footwear, at least some of the time (you'd be surprised how many people end up walking some of the way in their resting footwear).

Don't worry if your resting footwear doesn't meet all of these criteria; the main thing is comfort and lightness. It's entirely possible that you already own a pair of shoes that would fit the bill perfectly – and be well broken in.

There are many types of suitable footwear. **Flip-flops** (called **Thongs** in some countries) are very light and compact, but not everybody finds walking in them comfortable. **Crocs** and similar plastic shoes, are light, but again not everybody finds them comfortable. **Sandals** are great too and outdoor sandals such as those made by *Teva* are light and compact and you could actually hike in them (at least in good weather). **Light canvas shoes** like *Converse* are also good but not so well ventilated.

In the interests of full disclosure, I have to mention that I have never walked the Camino in anything other than Ecco boots and sandals (website global.ecco.com), and I have only once had reason to regret my choice. I'm now on my third pair of identical boots. I get about two Caminos from a pair before they stop being waterproof. Between pair two and three I digressed and bought a pair of Ecco boots of a slightly different and lighter design, but after about ten days walking I got pressure sores on the soles of my feet, mostly towards the end of the day. My holidays were over anyway, but this could have been a bit of a disaster had I been planning to go on. The lighter boots had less well cushioned soles, which I think caused the problem, and so I reverted to the old reliables for my next trip. My Ecco sandals serve as my resting footwear, despite being a bit on the heavy side. I think the extra weight is worth it because they're very comfortable to walk in. On hot days, I switch into them at about midday and carry my boots. On my first Camino, I wore my sandals exclusively for the final two weeks because my boots had become too tight. My next pair of boots I got one size bigger and they've been fine even on the longest Camino. Despite knowing exactly what works for me, I always time buying boots to break them in for at least six months before heading off on the Camino.

There is still a small number of hardy souls whose choice of footwear sets them apart from the common herd. I once met a guy from Luxembourg who walks the Camino every autumn wearing flip-flops. His choice of footwear didn't seem to be any impediment to him. But he did favour a particular brand of Brazilian flip-flops. One summer, I met an Irish guy walking in Converse. He said they were fine and he hadn't had a single blister. The prize for audacity goes to a Spanish guy I met on the Camino Mosarabé, during the Biblical deluge of May 2012. He was walking in his socks from

Granada, having made a promesa *that if his mother recovered from an illness he'd walk to Santiago* descalzado *(literally without shoes, although it's often translated as barefoot). He was doing fine, no major injuries, taking his time. The torrential rain wasn't affecting him any more than anybody else. He drew wonderful cartoons illustrating his progress and daily drenching in the* libros de peregrinos.

RAINWEAR

Most **modern rainwear** includes Gore-Tex or some other waterproof and breathable material. (For the technical low-down see page 142.) There are several options when it comes to rainwear and the most important factor is the time of year you'll be walking. In the **summer months** you can be minimalistic because you're unlikely to encounter long periods of heavy rain, wind and cold. **Outside of the summer months**, and the closer to January, the greater probability of needing serious rainwear that can also serve as cold weather wear.

WATERPROOF JACKET

A waterproof jacket is a good idea all year round, though in summer you could manage without one if you take a poncho instead. In summer a light jacket is fine but it should be loose-fitting so that you can wear layers under it on cold mornings and in the mountains. In the depths of winter, however, you will need a warm jacket.

A **good waterproof jacket** should ideally be a loose fit for layering. It should come to below your waist so water dripping down will mostly fall on the ground (looseness helps here too). It should fasten with a zip and have a flap which covers the zip when it's closed to prevent water seeping in, especially when walking into headwinds. It should have a hood with pull-strings to keep it in place on windy days. The collar should be sealable (if the zip doesn't go all the way up) to prevent water dripping in and heat escaping. The sleeves should also be sealable around the wrists to prevent heat loss. The zips should be sturdy and have big, easy to grip fasteners so you can work them while wearing gloves. It should have big pockets with zip fasteners and ideally a couple of inside pockets too. Sealable vents under the arms also help to regulate temperature. Finally, it should roll or fold small enough to fit in your backpack.

The quality of the material used is one factor in how much protection your jacket will give you from getting wet. Other factors include its general "build quality". Are seams tightly stitched and sealed? When you're wearing it with the hood up, does water drip down inside? Does water enter through pockets? Does it enter through zips? Does it enter underneath the straps of your backpack?

The **advantages** of a waterproof jacket are that it will help to keep you dry and warm. Because of its breathability, it's comfortable to wear in warm rain as well as cold. It won't flap around in the wind like a poncho and will be easier to put on and take off. It has pockets. It's good to wear if it gets cold in the evenings or even when you stop for a short break. It keeps your upper body dry and some of them even look nice (lets face it, in a poncho you'll look like a walking tent.)

The **disadvantages** are that they can be quite bulky to pack away, especially the winter ones, which is another reason why *layering* is such a good idea. In a prolonged downpour you'll more than likely discover the limits to its waterproofing as water may seep in through seams and under the waist and shoulder straps of your backpack.

However, a good jacket will still keep you fairly dry and warm despite a little seepage because its breathable qualities will help to expel any water that gets inside.

WATERPROOF PANTS (OR, IF YOU PREFER, *TROUSERS*)

Most pilgrims use the baggy waterproof pants which are designed to be worn as an extra layer over your normal clothes. Waterproof pants are excellent for cold and wet weather and in snow. In summer you might experience a couple of day of rain but it won't be very cold, so you could manage with shorts or light pants made of a quick-drying material. At other times of the year, the extra rain and cold protection will be important in the mountains, where you'll frequently encounter freezing temperatures.

Waterproof pants can be bought in the cheap plastic variety or the less-cheap Gore-Tex variety. They all do the waterproof thing, but if you want breathability you have to spend a bit more. Breathability is not as important as it is for jackets because (especially in cold weather) the lower half of your body won't sweat as much as the upper half.

Make sure the leg-bottoms are wide enough to allow you to put them on and take them off without having to remove your boots. Some models have a zip at the bottom of the leg which widens the opening enough to be able to take it off without a struggle.

There are also top-end waterproof pants made of advanced space-age materials which look like normal pants and are worn next to your skin and are not designed to be layered. These work well but are only really suitable for a mid-winter Camino.

The **advantages**; they'll keep your legs dry and warm in cold weather. They're not heavy (at least the plastics ones) and roll up fairly compactly.

The **disadvantages**; they're hot to wear unless it's freezing out. Getting into and out of them can be a pain.

PONCHOS

First of all, a clarification; this refers to "professional" ponchos, not to the cheap disposable ones which are designed to be used once and then thrown away.

Opinions vary greatly on the issue of ponchos, with some thinking they're the bee's knees and other people dismissing them as more trouble than they're worth. As previously stated, they can be ideal for a summer Camino instead of a waterproof jacket. They can also be an excellent addition to a waterproof jacket in the event of a prolonged period of rain.

A good poncho will cover your backpack completely and hang down to about your knees. It should be made of strong plastic, reinforced at the edges and at the neck (important point this) to prevent it ripping. It should have a hood with pull-strings so you can tighten it around your head. It should be light and pack away compactly

The **advantages**; they really will keep the rain off the top half of your body and your backpack. They dry pretty quickly and can even be worn still damp, without discomfort. In fact, if you get a plastic one all you have to do is shake it and it's dry. They usually pack up compactly and don't weigh much. You can get a good one for very little money.

The **disadvantages**; windy days, a poncho is difficult to get on and will flap all over the place, taking on alarming sail-like qualities when you eventually manage to get it on. (On the Camino the prevailing winds are westerlies, blowing in off the Atlantic straight into your face. And, as a general rule, when it blows, it rains). In warm weather you will get quite hot under your poncho and because they don't have the breathability of a good jacket you'll end up damp from sweat. In cold weather your poncho won't contribute much to keeping you warm. They're prone to snagging on bushes (and anything else).

I became a convert to ponchos late in life. It was October 2013, in Galicia. We'd already endured several days of miserable, cold rain blowing into our faces. At times it was so intense that even the locals were looking at the sky and shaking their heads. I'd spent the night in Palas de Rei, in a hotel, because I was feeling miserable. It was a cheap hotel and the heating wasn't on, so in the morning my clothes, boots, everything, was still damp. Over breakfast the television weather forecast revealed a complex interweaving of rain fronts forming an orderly queue, stretching half way across the Atlantic and moving at a leisurely pace in our direction like the horsemen of the Apocalypse.

And I still had three days to Santiago.

As I grimly headed back to the hotel I fought back tears, mortified in case anyone saw me having a "moment" at seven o'clock in the morning.

Trudging through the town I noticed a shop that was already open and doing a roaring trade, to judge by the number of pilgrims milling around inside. When I got closer I realised why. The mannequins in the window were all sporting ponchos! Gingerly I inspected the wares. They went from the flimsy disposable type to the ultra durable professional type. I contemplated for a moment before deciding I had nothing to lose and also that there was no point skimping (I'd bought cheap ponchos before and seen them shredded to ribbons before the day was over). So I got me the best and most expensive one they had – an Altus Atmospheric, hecho en España (made in Spain), 30€.

Within an hour I realised I was the owner of an impressive piece of raingear. It's shaped to fit over a backpack, has an adjustable hood, a good quality zip covered by a Velcro flap, and it comes down perfectly to my knees. It has wide sleeves which you can slip your arms into and out of as you please (almost like a Friar's robe). And, once you master the technique, it's easy to get into and out of; without your backpack you put the poncho on, and with your arms in the sleeves, you zip it up. Then you pull your arms inside and put your backpack on underneath the poncho.

It works really well. Having worn it for several days in heavy rain I can say it really keeps you dry, at least down as far as your knees. I'll never again go on a Camino, outside of the summer, without it. If I had to make one criticism it would be that the hood is a bit too big and falls over my face. However, wearing a baseball cap solves that problem perfectly.

It's changed my attitude to rain. When I wake in the morning and it's poring outside it doesn't bother me at all. I feel almost a state of bliss knowing that my wonderful poncho is going to get a day out and that other, less well prepared pilgrims will be staring at me in bewilderment and envy.

BACKPACK

Medium sized hiking backpacks, regardless of who makes them, are all based on a very similar design, and follow the principle that the weight in your pack should be carried by your hips rather than your shoulders. They have shoulder straps which are mostly for stability, a hip belt which takes most of the weight, an external rigid frame to keep the backpack upright and to allow the weight to be transferred down to you hips, and a mesh back panel which rests against your back while still allowing air to circulate between you and the backpack, to keep you cool on hot days. Backpack technology has evolved a lot in the past twenty or so years and a modern, well-fitting backpack is comfortable to carry, even when over-loaded. That doesn't mean you should over-load it! So, if the basic design of backpacks is more-or-less identical, what are the deciding factors when buying one?

The first thing is **size** (or more accurately **volume**). Backpack volume is generally measured in litres. Most pilgrims carry a backpack of about 40 litres. You can go smaller than this but generally, if this is your first time then 35 litres minimum is a good guideline. How big you go is up to you. Some people like loads of space and go for a 50 or 55 litre backpack. Which is fine, as long as the backpack itself doesn't weigh too much (see below) and as long as you can resist the temptation to fill it with stuff you don't need. (A bigger one can potentially be more useful, post-Camino, than a smaller backpack).

Next is **weight**. If you're aiming to keep your luggage under **7kg** (or whatever your target is), then you have to remember that that 7kg *includes* the weight of your backpack. If your backpack weighs 1.5kg, that only leaves you with 5.5kg for everything else. Some backpacks weigh 3kg or more, so remember to check the weight when choosing one.

Your backpack has to **fit** you. The straps are all adjustable so your size across the shoulders and hips doesn't make much difference. The height does. If you're tall you'll be more comfortable with a longer backpack. If you're short you can go for a shorter one. The base of the frame and the hip strap should rest on your hips. It shouldn't slip down as you move. At the same time, the shoulder straps should be comfortable around your shoulders, without being tight. Most of the weight should be on your hips, with very little on your shoulders. This is important; your shoulders are going to get sore if they have to carry a lot of weight for a long period. It's not going to do your spine any good either. The waist strap and the base of the backpack, should be cushioned to make carrying the weight on your hips comfortable. Finally, you really need to put something heavy in the backpack when trying it on, so you get the feel of what it's like fully loaded. Trying it on empty doesn't tell you much. Good outdoor shops will help you with this.

When you're satisfied with the basics - that it's big enough, light enough and it fits you - the remaining features are a matter of personal preference.

A **rain cover** is useful because most backpacks aren't waterproof. They usually come with one built in, but check anyway.

If you want to use a **water bladder** hydration system, make sure your choice of backpack accommodates it (most do, but check to make sure).

Different brands of backpack come with different **fasteners** to close the main compartment. Some have a string pull system with a flap to cover it to keep the rain out. Others have a zip. Both work fine.

Ease of access to the backpack's main compartment is determined by the **size of the opening** at the top. Many string pull backpacks have quite a small opening, and if you need to get something that's right down the bottom, often your only option is to unpack everything. This is inconvenient at best, and really inconvenient if you need your rainwear in the midst of a sudden downpour. Some backpacks have a **zip opening** at the top, which extends down the sides, so it can opens like a suitcase, allowing easy access to its inner depths. Whether this is an issue for you depends, to some degree, on how organised your packing is.

The question of **pockets** also boils down to preference and one's organisational habits. Some people love loads of external pocket, others find that it just makes it harder to find things. If you're the kind of person who always puts things in the same place, and will remember where that place is, then multiple pockets will probably suit you down to the ground. On the other hand, if you're someone who just tends to put things wherever is convenient, and then relies on serendipity to find them again, you might be better off forgetting about pockets and just relying on sticking everything in the main compartment (possibly in cloth or plastic bags). But please, please, please don't use plastic bags that make noise whenever you touch them, because at some stage or another you're going to have to search in them in the dead of night and will wake the whole dorm.

Backpacks aren't for everybody. I met a guy from Switzerland who was pushing a shopping trolley he'd bought in Pamplona with all his belongings in it. He'd had an accident and put his left shoulder out of joint and wasn't able to carry his backpack. The trolley was a nice orange colour, and it and its owner achieved almost celebrity-like status. On smooth surfaces he could push it in front of him, on rough he pulled it. He made it to Santiago and his arm was so improved that he was able to continue to Finisterre without the help of his trolley. He went on to achieve fame in his home country when a popular newspaper nominated him "Crazy Swiss Person of the Year", or something like that.

SLEEPING BAG / SLEEPING BAG LINER

What kind of sleeping bag you bring with you depends on what time of year you intend to walk. In **summer,** a light synthetic fibre one with a comfort range down to about 8°C is ideal (sometimes called *one season*). Some summer pilgrims go without a sleeping bag and instead bring a **sleeping bag liner**. A sleeping bag liner is similar to a sleeping bag except it's much lighter, often consisting of a single layer of material, usually cotton, silk or polyester, although they exist in a fleece version also.

The **advantages** of sleeping bag liners are that they're very lightweight, very compact, and cheap. On hot nights (and in hot stuffy dorms with little ventilation), they're more comfortable than a sleeping bag. Sleeping bag liners are also available pre-treated with bedbug repellent.

The **disadvantages** of sleeping bag liners are that they're really only suitable for hot nights, and even in summer it can get cold at night. Sometimes blankets are available in hostels, but this is by no means guaranteed, and if available, they may not be very clean. If you just bring a sleeping bag liner you may need to sleep in your clothes occasionally.

A sleeping bag liner, as its name suggests, can also be used inside a sleeping bag, where it will lower the minimum comfortable temperature by about 3 or 4 degrees.

In **winter,** a cold-weather sleeping bag (sometimes called *four seasons*) with a comfort range down to about freezing, is advisable.

Most modern **sleeping bags** are insulated with synthetic fibre although you can still find down (duck feather) filled ones. **Down** filled sleeping bags are warmer for their weight, but if they get wet they're very difficult to dry. You can wash them in a washing machine, but they have to be dried on a flat surface, or the distribution of feathers inside the bag becomes uneven. **Synthetic fibre** sleeping bags are slightly bulkier, but will still keep you warm even when wet and will dry a lot faster. They can also be tumble dried.

Most sleeping bags are *Mummy* shaped; they get narrower towards your feet, and have a hood for your head. If you find this claustrophobic, you can still find the old-style square ones, which have the added advantages of allowing you to open the zip at the bottom and stick your feet out to keep cool, and to open the zip completely and use it like a blanket.

Sleeping bags usually come with a storage bag (sometimes called a stuff-sack). Sometimes the manufacturer recommends rolling it before putting it into its bag, other times they just tell you to stuff it in. Have a look at the label before you throw it away.

Also, pay attention the the dimensions of the sleeping-bag, especially if you're tall, broad shouldered, or broad anything else too.

I've had a variety of light sleeping bags down the years, which always did me fine on the Camino Francés. However, for my first trip on the Vía de la Plata in winter, I really suffered. All I had was a summer sleeping bag, and it was cold in the dorms at night and there were no blankets. I ended up wearing all my clothes (including my rainwear) inside my sleeping bag and I still froze. When I got home, I splashed out on a duck feather sleeping bag from an Army Surplus Store, which is absolutely amazing to sleep in (like checking into a four-star hotel, minus the mini-bar!) and warm enough down to about freezing point. The only disadvantage is that it is hard to dry once it gets wet. After I wash it I lay it flat on the back seat of my car and park it in the sun, and even then it takes a couple of days to dry (I live in Dublin, and sunny days are rare). My summer sleeping bag is from Deuter (who also make the most popular brand of backpacks among non-Spanish pilgrims). Its label says it has a Comfort temperature of 12°C, with a Limit of 8°C, and in my experience that's fairly accurate. It packs very neatly, weighs a couple of hundred grammes and only cost about 50€.

TOWEL

Most pilgrims carry a lightweight, quick-drying pack (AKA *microfibre*) towel, rather than a traditional cotton towel. Although, for only a small bit of extra weight, you could bring a small conventional towel. Just bear in mind that getting it dry in winter might be difficult.

The **advantages** of a pack towel over a traditional one are that it dries quickly, it's light and rolls up very small. In fact, after wringing it out it's dry enough to use again. The only **disadvantage** is that the feel of pack towel on your skin isn't a particularly pleasant experience, and drying yourself with one require more patting than rubbing. Not everybody's cup of tea.

MONEY BELT / DOCUMENT POUCH / TRAVEL WALLET

The tradition **money belt** isn't popular on the Camino because of the heat. Basically, it will make you feel hotter and it will get soaked with sweat. **Pouches** that you hang around your neck are more popular and give some protection for their content from rain, however, they don't always combine well with a backpack from a comfort point-of-view, and they are also a bit obvious. **Bum (Fanny) Bags** work too and, worn at the front, have the advantage of being easily accessible. Again, it's obvious where you valuables are and they mightn't combine well with a backpack. A **Travel Wallet** may also be useful, although there isn't much to distinguish it from a normal wallet.

For your documents, you need something big enough to hold your passport and a Credencial (see page 38., the traditional *Amis du Chemin* Credencial issued in Saint-Jean, is 17cm x 10cm, Spanish ones are slightly smaller) and whatever else you need to keep safe and dry, not just from the rain but also if you want to keep it with you when you take a shower.

You need something that you're comfortable carrying and that isn't too obvious. I used to use a pouch hung around my neck but I found it irritating and uncomfortable at times and on one occasion I lost it because I took it off when I stopped for a break. After that I started wearing pants with secure zippy pockets, one for my wallet and one for my passport and Credencial, with cards split between the two. It works well for me, it's comfortable, secure and discreet. You just have to have the pocket requirement is mind when you go pants shopping.

EAR PLUGS

Some people are deep sleepers and manage fine without ear plugs. The rest of us like to have them handy for encounters with those legendary creatures who can keep not just a whole dorm awake, but a whole hostel, and possibly the neighbours too.

There are several kinds of noise reducing ear plugs made of foam or wax. The wax ones, if they fit correctly, offer the best noise reduction. Using them is easy, hold two in your hand until they soften, mould them into the shape you want and insert them in your ears. They're reusable. The foam ones are made of mouldable (or memory) foam and just go straight in your ears. Some are single use and some are reusable.

If you've never used ear plugs before, try out a few different kinds to find out which are the best for you.

Stash a pair of ear plugs under your pillow when you go to bed so you'll be able to find them if you need them. But don't stash all your ear plugs there because you're bound to forget them at some stage.

TOILETRIES

Most pilgrims use hard **soap**. It has the advantage of being small, light and long-lasting. You can use it for hand-washing clothes as well as yourself. It's commonly available, even in the smallest village. It can be a bit messy in your backpack, so you'll need to store it in a sealable, waterproof container or a mesh bag so you can hang it out to dry after using it.

Hardcore hikers and cyclists sometimes cut the handle off their **toothbrush** to save a couple of grams. It makes washing your teeth a lot harder though.

Nail clippers; long toe nails can cause problems for your feet.

Toothpaste, toothbrushes, soap, and any hygiene and toiletry products you might need are widely available along the Camino route. In villages you won't get much of a selection but you'll get all the basics. In supermarkets in larger towns all the major European brands are available. The content of your toilet bag is up to you, and really won't be so different from a normal holiday, except that you'll have to keep things to a bare minimum and, if possible, go for smaller packets.

SUN SCREEN

For more information about sun screen see page 63.

PASSPORT / ID

By law, you must have your Passport (or ID card, if you're from an EU country that issues them) on you at all times. You may be asked to show it when checking in to some of the bigger municipal hostels.

MONEY / CASH AND CREDIT CARD

See, Banking and Money, page 57.

CREDENCIAL

See, The Credencial / Pilgrim Passport, page 38.

CLOTHES

Materials for clothes As a general rule, any item of clothing you bring with you should be hard-wearing, light and easy to pack away compactly. It's also important that it does not absorb a lot of water, keeps you warm even when damp and is quick drying. This mostly confines you to synthetic fabrics. Polyester is a good example of a material with these qualities. This type of material is sometimes also referred to as *Tech* or *Technical*. A natural alternative to artificial fibres is Merino wool, which is popular for sports clothing because it naturally draws moisture away from the wearer's skin (in a process known as *wicking*). It's soft and light and keeps its insulating properties even when wet.

Denim and other types of wool, are too heavy and take an eternity to dry in cold or damp weather. Cotton socks or underwear are OK as long as you have a few spare pairs. Cotton T-shirts and shirts will dry quickly in summer, but after a few days of rain (which can happen in summer too) you may end up wishing you'd gone for those synthetic fabrics or Merino.

Dark colours will be easier to keep clean-looking when all that's available for laundry is a sink with cold water. However, they will absorb more heat from direct sun.

SOCKS

On the subject of socks there are several schools of thought, and little consensus. Some pilgrims go for **sports** or **running socks**, available in outdoor shops. These are usually made of thin, fast-drying wool, and may have extra cushioning in vulnerable spots and / or double layers of material to reduce friction. There are also specialised **hiking socks**. Other pilgrims (and this seems to be a Nordic peculiarity) wear **two pairs** of thin socks together, possibly combining wool and silk. The logic being that wearing two socks reduces friction on your skin. Other pilgrims take a minimalist approach and wear **light sports socks** or even **everyday socks**.

Three pairs of socks is a good number to bring since you mightn't always be able to get them dry in one day. One (or even two) more pairs gives you a bit of extra leeway.

I always wear cheap everyday socks made of a mixture of cotton and polyester (approx 70/30), the same kinds I wear at home. In my experience, if you get your boots right you don't have to worry about your socks. I usual bring four pairs and if they're not dry in the morning, I tie them to the outside of my backpack, like a mobile clothes-line.

UNDERWEAR

Most pilgrims go for standard cotton undies, which do the job perfectly well. More technically sophisticated underwear is available from sports and outdoor stores, which may dry more quickly or keep you slightly cooler.

Most female pilgrims wear sports bras. When choosing what to bring make sure it works together with your backpack.

For men, although the extra ventilation of boxer-shorts may be nice on a hot day, the extra support of more conventional briefs may be more comfortable over time. Two pairs should be enough, but an extra one might be wise. In winter, you could consider a mix of normal and thermal undies.

The most important consideration is comfort when you're walking long distances.

GLOVES

Useful to have in summer as well as winter. They weigh very little and don't take up space and you could be very glad of them if you hit some cold weather in the mountains (especially if you want to use walking poles).

FLEECE

Even in summer, you'll need something warm for evenings or early morning. A fleece is ideal, but really you can take anything that's capable of being combined in layers with your other upper body wear, to give you warmth when you need it.

PANTS, ETC.

The ideal pair of pants for a summer Camino will be made of a light, hard-wearing, quick-drying material, and be light in colour to reflect heat from the sun. In summer, most pilgrims walk in shorts and have a second pairs of pants for when it's cool in the evening. Hiking pants with zip-off lower legs are a useful alternative to bringing shorts. In winter, pilgrims generally wear heavier pants for walking and have a pair of tracksuit bottoms for evenings and possibly also for sleeping in.

In summer, some women walk in skirts (and occasionally summer dresses), as an alternative to shorts. Naturally, a gentleman can avail of the benefits of skirt-wearing by attiring himself in a kilt, and at the same time, acquire a cachet of Sean Connery-like sophistication.

Leggings are also popular all year round for walking wear or evening wear.

Whatever you preference, take into consideration whether it has pockets, whether the pockets have zips, and whether they're big enough to be useful for carrying things you're likely to need frequently.

T-SHIRT / SHIRT

Whether you go for T-shirts or shirts (or one of each) is a personal preference. Shirts have the advantage of allowing air to circulate more freely around your body to keep you cool. The collar will protect your neck from the sun. The sleeves will protect your arms. In cold weather, it offers a little more protection from the cold because it can be buttoned up and tucked in your pants. It can also be worn between a T-shirt and a fleece on really cold days. Shirts made of synthetic material will dry in a flash and don't look like they haven't been ironed.

HAT

Ideally you need one hat which can protect you from the sun, the rain and, at other times, keep your head warm. That may be too much to ask of one hat, so in summer consider something with a wide brim, to keep the sun off, ventilation holes, and a chin-strap so it can't blow away on windy days. In winter a "woolly" hat of some description, will keep you head and ears warm.

SCARF / NECK WARMER

Protecting your throat from the cold can be difficult on days with a cold wind blowing in your face. **Scarves** aren't that useful on the Camino because they're bulky and don't fit well with a waterproof jacket with a tight collar. A **neck warmer** is a tube of material which you wear around your neck or which can also double as a hat. It's compact and light. It's also useful as a blindfold against emergency exit lights (which many hostels have been installing in dorms in recent years, and which stay on all night). A subspecies of neck warmer is the **bandanna**, which with its multiple uses on neck and head, is a possible alternative to a hat in summer.

WATERBOTTLE

You'll need storage for at least a litre of water and preferably two. There are two main schools of thought on "rehydration solutions": the waterbottle and the bladder.

Waterbottles come in all shapes, sizes and colours, but the main categories are plastic and metal. **Plastic waterbottles** are made of hard plastic. The size of the drinking opening varies, larger ones are easier to fill (especially in a shallow sink) but also easier to spill. They're closed with a plastic screw-on top, which should be attached to the bottle in some way, so you don't lose it. They're usually transparent so you can see how much water is in them, it also makes it easier to inspect the interior. Modern *Nalgene* waterbottles claim to be unbreakable and probably are. The main **disadvantage** of large-opening bottles is that you have to stand still to drink from them or risk pouring half of it over yourself.

Metal waterbottles look a bit like a flask with a small, screw-on top. This smaller opening makes them easier to drink from while walking (although you still need to look where you're going). Their interior is coated with a material which prevents the build up of bacteria. They're pretty tough and it would take a real effort to put a dent in one. Their main disadvantage is that you can't see how much water is in there or, for that matter, what else. Also, not everybody is comfortable with the sensation of drinking from a metal container.

Bladders are clear, flexible plastics sacks with a screw-on top, with a hose attached with a "bite valve" which the user drinks from. The bladder is normally stored in your backpack (most modern backpacks have a special compartment to hold it, and a hole to run the hose through). The pressure exerted by the weight of the contents of your backpack should place the water in the bladder under sufficient pressure that when you open the bite valve with your teeth to drink, the water should squirt out of its own accord. The **advantages** of bladders are that you don't have to stop to drink, so you can drink small quantities more frequently, which is the recommended way to avoid dehydration. You can keep your water cooler, because it's in your backpack away from direct sunlight. There are no **disadvantages** to this system really, except perhaps that it discourages you from taking your time.

I've tried all of the above at different times and, in the end, I concluded the handiest thing is two one litre plastic bottles (mineral water, Coke, etc.). They're widely available and zero maintenance. I fill them with tap water and put them in the mesh side pockets of my backpack. They're light, transparent, and they last about a month before they start looking unsightly. I wash them out daily to prevent build-up of bacteria. Plus, stretching your arm back to get one, without taking your backpack off, is a great exercise for your shoulder joints!

Packing: Other equipment

Walking poles: They will, if used properly, take some of the strain of walking off your leg muscles and joints, and make downhill sections easier on you knees. So, if you're worried about that, or if you have a history of knee problems, it might be worth your while trying them. The best way to learn how to use them (it's not as obvious as you might think!) is to join a *Nordic Walking* group near where you live. Or search for videos on the internet. They also may help to reduce swelling in your hands, a non-serious condition which affects some people as a reaction to the heat. If you're not concerned about your knees and don't specifically want to exercise your upper body, then don't bother with them.

My own experience with walking poles has been mixed. I tried them for one Camino and, they definitely did make it easier on my legs. However, I found if I used them all day I ended up with a sharp pain at the base of my neck. So, it was a toss up between that and sore knees. As a compromise, I used them some of the time, and mostly on downhill sections. So they spent most of the time strapped to my backpack. More recently I haven't bothered to bring them because I manage without them, and because you can't take them as hand-luggage on internal EU flights.

The old pilgrim hostel in Roncesvalles used to have a pilgrim "swap shop" area where you could leave things you'd figured out you didn't need after your first day's walking, and take stuff other people had abandoned. Among the tents, inflatable mattresses and camping stoves gathering dust, there was always a couple of walking poles. I didn't feel tempted.

Many pilgrims bring them but most don't know how to use them correctly and end up walking along tapping the ground with them. So, if you want to try them, take the time to learn the technique.

Bandages: specifically, tubular support bandages for your knees or ankles. These can be surprisingly helpful in easing minor joint pain. They don't weigh much or take up much space, so they might be good to have if you're worried about your joints.

Torch / Flashlight: Can be useful for finding your way to the bathroom late at night, though most hostels now have emergency exit lights which never go out. If you're walking in winter it makes more sense to have one. It's worth investing in a good quality torch; the cheap ones just break quickly. Check the on switch can't be pressed by accident when it's packed away or else when you need it the battery will be run down. Most smartphones have a built-in torch (also acts as a flash).

Sunglasses: Great to have in summer if you're in any way sensitive to bright sunlight.

Sleeping mat: Cheap, light and very handy if you have to sleep on the ground or outside (always a possibility in Galicia in July and August). Also great for siestas / picnics, etc.

Cutlery (knife / fork / spoon): Camino kitchens tend to have lots of cutlery, until you arrive in Galicia. However, if you like to have picnics, a knife and spoon are handy.

Zippy Bags / Baggies: These sealable plastic bags come in different sizes and are excellent for keeping your passport, Credencial and other bits and pieces dry. They can also be used for general organisation of different categories of equipment and (hopefully) preventing complete chaos in your backpack.

Bathing Suit (or whatever you want to call them): In summer many Camino villages have a public open-air swimming pool. Occasionally there are opportunities for river swimming. However, you're better off sticking to the approved places, signposted as *Playa Fluvial*.

Hankies / Kleenex: It's handy to have a small supply, but they are easily bought in almost any small shop.

Plastic Bin Bags / Trash Bags: These weigh almost nothing and take no space but they're great for "ultimate waterproofing". No matter how wet the weather, if you line your backpack with one of these you can feel confident that at the end of the day you'll have dry clothes to change into and a dry sleeping bag to curl up in. Well worth it!

Medical Kit: It's handy to have basic pain killers, plasters, etc. and possibly a basic blister treatment kit (Compeed, needle, thread, disinfectant). However, it isn't worth your while bringing a lot of medical supplies. Just about everything you could possibly need will be available from Pharmacies along the Camino.

Plastic sheet: For sleeping outside, 2m x 2m. Not as good as a tent but much cheaper and will protect you from rain, dew, bird droppings, creepy-crawlies and nosy sheep.

Mobile phone: If staying in contact is important. Bring one with a good battery life and save on the hassle of finding a place to charge it every day. If it's got WiFi you can use it for emailing, etc. Or get yourself a Spanish SIM card (see page 59).

Multi-socket adaptor: Electricity outlets are often in short supply in hostels. An adaptor which allows you to plug in more than one device at a time can save you waiting around for an outlet to become free.

Camping stove: You won't save much money by cooking for yourself and you'll have the added weight of stove, food, plates, etc. If you want / need to cook for yourself, most of the time (except in Galicia) it's possible to plan your stages to only stop at hostels with kitchens.

Tent: Unless you're determined to sleep outside, this is a complete waste of space. The law in Spain relating to wild camping varies from region to region. However, it is always prohibited near historic buildings and main roads.

Clothes line: Basically, a piece of string, although camping shops sell more professional ones. Handy at busy times.

Clothes pegs: These are handy to have because often they're in limited supply at hostels. Try to get a distinctive design or colour so you'll know which are yours.

Duct tape: Useful for emergency repairs to just about anything. It also works well as friction protection on heels. Better still, Gaffer Tape doesn't leave a sticky residue and is easier to handle.

Umbrella: Useful against rain and sun. Not much use in strong winds.

Net clothes bag: To keep your clothes together if you're sharing a washing machine with other pilgrims.

Hi-Viz Jacket: A yellow reflective jacket (like the ones cyclists wear) makes you more visible to drivers in winter when days are short and possibly dull.

Sealable food container (*Tupperware*): This is useful if you're preparing your own meals. Leftovers become tomorrow's lunch.

Camera: More and more pilgrims are using the camera on their phone, but if you want to take good photos a proper camera is essential. Digital cameras use rechargeable Ni-MH batteries, most of them don't work well with disposable batteries. If you don't want to carry a charger, you'll need, either to carry a supply of charged batteries or to get a camera with a build-in charger.

Gaiters: These waterproof covers which fasten around your ankle and lower leg, protecting against water and mud, are useful in winter to stop water going in over the top of your boot and protect the legs of your pants from mud.

Notebook and pen: Making notes, taking people's emails, drawing pictures. Keeping a diary can be a nice souvenir of the Camino.

I have a list in a spreadsheet of everything I need for a Camino. It varies a little for summer and winter, but not much. I print it out a few weeks before departure and mark out the items I need to buy. Then, a few days before departure, I start assembling everything. Once it's packed, it's crossed off the list. That way I know I haven't forgotten anything, and that I haven't packed things I won't need. You can download a sample list from caminoguide.net/packing.

How to get to the Camino

Possible starting points are listed in Camino order (apart from places which aren't on the Camino, which are at the end). Look up the place you want to start, and you'll find a description of how to get there. General information about booking trains, buses and flights as well as useful websites is in **Booking travel online** (Page 31).

Departure times given are subject to change. Please check on the company's website for your travel dates.

The Spanish for *Bus Station* is *Estación de Autobuses* and *Train Station* is *Estación de Tren* although the word *Ferrocarril / Railway* is also used.

Students and people under 26 often qualify for discounts on train and bus tickets. When booking online look out for Spanish *estudiante* or French *étudiant*. When travelling, you will need to have proof of your age and / or a student card. Often a national student ID won't be enough; you'll need an internationally recognised one. Ask your Students Union or college for more details.

If you're planning to walk the "whole Camino" starting in Saint-Jean-Pied-de-Port you will either need to pass through Bayonne on the French side or Pamplona on the Spanish.

ARRIVING FROM OUTSIDE EUROPE

If you're arriving from outside Europe you'll probably be flying into one or other hub airports. From the perspective of getting to the Camino, each has its advantages and disadvantages.

London has four airports. Intercontinental flights arrive into Heathrow from where there are connection flights to destinations around Europe. Flights to Biarritz (and many other airports in France and Spain) also leave from Stansted (*Ryanair*) or Gatwick (*Easyjet*). Stansted and Gatwick are both about a two-hour bus ride from Heathrow. Bus tickets can be bought from *www.nationalexpress.com*. For the return journey there are flights to one or other of the London airports from many Spanish cities, including Santiago.

Madrid has one airport, *Barajas*. There are some direct buses from the airport to many towns along the Camino, including Pamplona. However, there are more frequent services from the city centre bus station on *Avenida de las Americas,* and train services from either Atocha or Chamartín train stations. Getting back to Madrid from Santiago you have the choice of train, bus or airplane.

Paris has two airports but most intercontinental flights arrive into *Paris Charles de Gaulle* (formerly called *Roissy*). From here there are connecting flights to Bayonne with *Air France.* There are also trains from the airport train station to Bayonne, although you may have to change in Bordeaux. If you need to go to a starting point in Spain, you'll need to get the same train to *Hendaye* and change to a Spanish train there. Getting back to Paris, your options are a train from Hendaye or Madrid, or a plane from Santiago (with *Vueling*) or Madrid (various airlines).

Dublin has one airport with flights from North America with *Aer Lingus, American Airlines* and *United Airlines,* and from Abu Dhabi on *Etihad*. Onward flights are available to Biarritz with *Ryanair,* or various destinations in Spain with *Ryanair* or *Aer Lingus.* Flights back from Santiago are available with *Aer Lingus* or from Madrid with *Ryanair* or *Aer Lingus.*

TOWNS ON THE CAMINO

SAINT-JEAN-PIED-DE-PORT

This is the traditional start of the Camino Francés. The easiest way to get to Saint-Jean from other parts of France is to go to Bayonne (Page 30) and get the **train** from there. There are four trains a day taking about one hour. A one-way ticket costs about 11€. As this is a local train, there are no seat reservations and you don't need to buy tickets in advance. For local train information in south west France, see *www.ter-sncf.com/aquitaine*. Click in the top right corner to change the language. Now click *Ticket & train status,* and *Timetables...* (If a *choose your country* window pops up just close it by clicking on the *x* in the top right.) Now in *From* enter (for example) *Bayonne* and in *To* enter *Saint-Jean-Pied-de-Port*. Enter the date you want to travel, change the departure time to sometime early in the morning so you get all of the day's trains, and click search. (**NOTE**: engineering works during summer 2015 have ended and this train service is now running normally)

If you're coming from Spain, during the summer there is a **direct bus service** from Pamplona bus station run by the company **Alsa** – website *www.alsa.es*. It leaves weekdays at 10:00, 12:00, 14:30 and 17:30. Cost 22€. Please check the timetable on their website for your travel date.

Express Bourricot runs a taxi / shuttle bus to Saint-Jean from Biarritz airports. For information and reservations, see their website *www.expressbourricot.com*

Taxis in Pamplona will happily take a fare to Saint-Jean. It should cost about 100€ (125€ at weekends) for up to four passengers.

RONCESVALLES

The only way to get to Roncesvalles from the Spanish side is through Pamplona. The bus service run by Alsa from Pamplona to Saint-Jean-Pied-de-Port stops in Roncesvalles. See more details under Saint-Jean-Pied-de-Port.

The only other option is a **taxi**. The taxi fare from Pamplona to Roncesvalles is about 60€ (a little more at weekends).

If you want to get to Roncesvalles from the French side (without walking), then Express Bourricot offers a taxi and shuttle bus service. See under Saint-Jean-Pied-de-Port.

Roncesvalles website: *www.roncesvalles.es*

PAMPLONA

There are no international flights into **Pamplona airport**. The nearest major airports are Bilbao and Madrid.

There are several **trains** a day from **Madrid Atocha** railway station to Pamplona. It's a pleasant journey and takes about three hours. The price varies according to how long in advance you book, and starts at about 25€ for 2nd class. There are also two trains a day from Hendaye/Irún. See the RENFE website.

There are **bus services** from points within Spain including Madrid, Hendaye, Bilbao, etc. Pamplona's super-modern bus station is underground and is accessible via a glass building on *Calle Yanguas y Miranda,* with *Estación de Autobuses* etched in tiny letters on the glass (you can easily walk past it and not see it). See *www.estaciondeautobusesdepamplona.com*

PUENTE LA REINA

Puente is easily accessible from Pamplona. **Buses** from Pamplona leave from the bus station and stop in Puente on the main road parallel to *Calle Mayor.* They are operated by Conda, *www.conda.es.*

ESTELLA

There are **buses** from Pamplona, San Sebastian, Hendaye, etc. They arrive at the bus station on *Calle de Sancho El Sabio.*

LOGROÑO

There is one **train** a day from Madrid arriving in the evening, taking about 3½ hours, prices from about 25€.

Buses run from Pamplona, Burgos, San Sebastian, Madrid, etc, to the *Estación de Autobuses* on *Avenida de España.* Local buses run to points throughout La Rioja and southern Navarra.

BURGOS

One problem with **trains** in Burgos is that the train station (*Burgos Rosa De Lima*) is an inconveniently long way outside the city. That said, there are several trains a day from Madrid, taking about 2½ hours. If you're coming from Paris, the Madrid-Paris sleeper train stops here in the early morning. It takes about ten hours from Paris.

There are **bus services** from all major cities in Spain. The bus station is directly across the river from the Cathedral square, only about a five minute walk. The bus from Madrid is faster and cheaper than the train. The express bus, which use the motorway, takes about 2 hours and cost about 20€. Local buses to places in Burgos province and parts of La Rioja also arrive at the bus station.

SAHAGÚN

Sahagún is a stop on the León-Madrid **railway,** with several trains a day in both directions. From Madrid it takes between 2 and 3 hours and to León it takes less than an hour (about 3 days walking!)

There are also **buses** from León which stop on the main road near the Camino.

MANSILLA DE LAS MULAS

Buses from León arrive at the bus station, which is just south of the town centre.

LEÓN

There are several **trains** a day from Madrid, taking about three hours; one a day from Santiago, taking five hours, and one from Hendaye via San Sebastian, taking five hours. There's also one train from Bilbao, taking five hours. The railway station is across the river from the city centre. NB: The narrow-gauge train line between Bilbao and León has closed.

Buses from throughout Spain arrive at the bus station, as do local buses from around the Province of León. The bus station is near the railway station on the banks of the river, on the opposite side to the city centre.

ASTORGA

Astorga is one stop down the **train** line from León and has basically the same services.

There are frequent **bus** services from León, taking about an hour.

PONFERRADA

Ponferrada is on the same **train** line as Astorga and León, with direct connections from Madrid taking about five hours. The train station is across the river from the municipal hostel, on *Avenida el Castillo*.

There are regular **bus** services from Santiago de Compostela, Madrid, León, etc. The bus station is on *Avenida de Asturias*.

SARRIA

Buses from Santiago to Sarria are run by the company *Monbus* (or *Monforte*), Monday to Friday at 18:00, taking two and a half hours and leaving from the Bus Station in Santiago. See. *www.monbus.es*. If this doesn't suit you, the easiest way to get to Sarria is through Lugo (Page 31).

SANTIAGO DE COMPOSTELA

If you're planning to walk the last 100km, your easiest option may be to fly into Santiago and get a direct bus (or one via Lugo) to Sarria.

There are **direct flights** to Santiago from several European cities including Basel, Dublin, Frankfurt/M, Geneva, Istanbul, London, Milan, Paris and Zurich. There are also direct flights from Caracas in Venezuela. The Tourist Information website *www.santiagoturismo.com/como-chegar/en-avion* has more detailed information.

There's an overnight **train** to and from **Madrid** with **couchettes** (beds) available for an extra charge. They are highly recommended if you want to get some decent sleep.

There's also a daily train between Santiago and **Hendaye**, calling at Ponferrada, Astorga, León, Sahagún, Burgos, San Sebastian and Hendaye. A couple of carriages split off to go to Bilbao. It leaves Santiago around 10:00 (tends to vary a bit!), and takes eleven hours to get to Hendaye.

From the **bus station** on *Avenida de Rodriguez de Viguri* there are buses to all major destinations in Galicia and Spain. The bus to **Finisterre** leaves from here and takes about three hours. This journey can be an unpleasant experience for those who suffer from travel sickness. The bus to **Sarria** also leave from the bus station. There are also buses to Porto in Portugal.

There are **buses to the airport** from various points around town. However, all services call at the main bus station on the way so getting the bus from there is probably the safest option. Check with **Tourist Information** just to be sure.

FINISTERRE / FISTERRA
There are several **buses** a day between Finisterre and Santiago. The bus-stop in Finisterre is right beside the Xunta hostel. The bus follows different routes at different times and takes up to three hours.

Finisterre **taxi drivers** will take up to four people straight to Santiago for about 80€, taking about an hour. The taxi rank is just down the street from the Xunta hostel (Finisterre is pretty small). Santiago taxi drivers will usually do a run in the opposite direction for about the same price.

MUXÍA
There are several **buses** a day between Muxía and Santiago, taking about two hours. The bus-stop in Muxía is on the waterfront.

TOWNS NOT ON THE CAMINO

BAYONNE (AND BIARRITZ)
Biarritz airport is a local bus ride from Bayonne railway station on **Bus C,** or the slightly more circuitous **Bus 14**. Cost 1€. Several airlines fly here from destinations around Europe (there are no flights from outside Europe), including Birmingham, Bournemouth, Brussels (Charleroi), Copenhagen, Dublin, Geneva, Helsinki, Lille, London (Stansted and Gatwick), Lyon, Marseilles, Nice, Paris, Rotterdam and Stockholm and Strasbourg. See a full list at *en.biarritz.aeroport.fr*

If you're coming from Paris, there are frequent **TGV (high-speed train)** connections from *Paris Monparnasse* station and less frequent ones from *Paris Charles de Gaulle* airport. Some are direct and others require a change in Bordeaux. They take between five and seven hours.

If you're coming from Spain by train you'll go to Hendaye first, then get the train to Bayonne.

By bus there are several services a day from Pamplona and San Sebastian run by Alsa. They pass either through Hendaye or Sant-Jean-Pied-de-Port. See *www.alsa.es*

Volunteers based in Bayonne cathedral provide help and advice to pilgrims during the summer months. They can advise on accommodation in Bayonne and on the Camino del Baztán (see page 79).

BILBAO

Bilbao airport has flights from destinations throughout Europe. See *www.bilbaoair.com/aeropuerto-bilbao-destinos-03.htm*

There are **trains** on the regional **EuskoTren** network from Santander, San Sebastian and Hendaye, where you can connect to the French train network (see under Hendaye below). Although, a warning, EuskoTren is slow, the bus is often faster.

The **bus** from the airport to the city centre terminates at the bus station, from where there are frequent connections to Pamplona, León, etc.

HENDAYE (AND IRÚN)

Situated on the French side of the French / Spanish border opposite Irún, Hendaye is important as the meeting point between the French and Spanish train networks. Because French and Spanish trains have different gauges, most of them terminate here (except the Madrid-Paris overnight trains, which have adjustable axles). The French SNCF and the Spanish Basque regional EuskoTren railway stations are right beside each other in Hendaye. The RENFE mainline Spanish railway station is just across the border in Irún.

From Madrid and other parts of Spain including Pamplona, there are RENFE **trains**. EuskoTren connects Santander, Bilbao and San Sebastian, see *www.euskotren.es*. EuskoTren is slow and often the bus is faster.

There are regular **bus** services from Pamplona, San Sebastian, Bilbao and Biarritz Airport.

SANTANDER

Santander airport has flights from destinations in western Europe including Brussels (Charleroi), Dublin, Edinburgh, Frankfurt/M, London (Stansted), Milan, Paris, and Rome. A bus from the airport drops off in the city centre.

Ferries arrive here from various southern English ports.

From Santander there are **bus** services to major towns on the Camino such as Pamplona, Burgos and León.

Train run from Santander to Madrid passing through Palancia from where you could get to Camino towns such as Frómista or Carrión de los Condes.

LUGO

There are two **trains** a day from Madrid to Lugo, one leaving around noon and taking about sever hours, and an overnight one which leaves in the evening. There's also an overnight train from Barcelona, taking 13 hours.

If you're coming from Santiago, there are frequent **buses** to Lugo taking about two hours. They arrive at the bus station, where you can change to a local bus to Sarria, which runs about every hour and takes about 30 minutes.

Booking travel online

Most of the websites listed have an **English version** (of varying quality). If the link brings up a page in Spanish or French, there is usually a list of national flags or a drop-down list to change the language. Booking in advance over the internet, for both trains and planes, often gets you a cheaper fare. Sometimes a lot cheaper. Tickets bought **last minute or at the station** nearly always cost more.

TRAINS

Long distance **trains** have first and second class compartments. Tickets for these trains can be bought online, or at the station up to a few minutes before departure. However, if you buy in advance you're more likely to get a good price. The best discounts (as much as 70%) can be obtained by booking at least two months in advance. At busy times (weekends, holidays and July and August), it's advisable to book well in advance because trains are often full. For most journeys, it's possible to book up to three months in advance.

Reserving a seat is usually mandatory when buying a ticket for long-distance trains. In Spain the reservation is part of the ticket. However, in France it is separate. When buying online you'll be forced to reserve, if it's mandatory. If you're buying a ticket that involves **changing trains** or **crossing a national border,** be sure to ask for reservations for all the parts of the journey on which it's required.

Tickets for **local trains** (such as the one from Bayonne to Saint-Jean-Pied-de-Port), can be bought on the day of travel from the ticket office in the station without any price penalty. There are no seat reservations on local trains.

For **everything you ever wanted to know about travelling by train in Europe,** see *The Man in Seat 61* at *www.seat61.com*. If you're new to European train travel (or even if you're an old hand) this website is an invaluable information resource.

FRANCE

In France, **trains** are fast and reliable, if a little expensive. The train company is called **SNCF,** and its reservations website is *www.voyages-sncf.com*. To get the website in English, the option to change the language is in the top right. You can buy and print tickets from this website or optionally select to collect the tickets from the station on the day of travel.

There are several classes of train, from the high-speed, long-distance *TGV* (*Trains à Grande Vitesse*), which includes *Eurostar* services to London, to the slower, long-distance *Téoz* and the *Intercités de Nuit* (also sometimes called *TEN – Trans Euro Nuit*) night trains with optional sleeping compartments (*Couchettes*). Then there are local trains, which are slower and make frequent stops.

SNCF operates a US-based subsidiary, which runs the ***www.raileurope.com*** website, and you may be redirected to this website when you specify your country on *www.voyages-sncf.com*. The problem with this is that *www.raileurope.com* doesn't always show the cheaper fares, so be sure to compare both websites before buying.

For more detailed information about rail travel in France have a look at: *www.seat61.com/France.htm*

In France **intracity bus services** are rare, and generally only exist where there is no train service. They are often run by SNCF.

SPAIN

The train company in Spain is called **RENFE** and its website, *www.renfe.com*, allows you to check timetables and buy and print tickets. Buying in advance is cheaper and advisable because trains are often full at peak times. To switch languages, select 'Welcome' from the top of the screen. Unfortunately, the English translation is incomplete. RENFE has first and second class, called *Preferente* and *Turista*.

In the Basque Country, there's a regional train network called **EuskoTren**, which has a line linking Hendaye, Irún and San Sebastián. This is a local, commuter service and you can't book in advance. Trains are frequent but slow.

For more detailed information about rail travel in Spain have a look at: *www.seat61.com/Spain.htm*

Intercity bus services in Spain are generally reliable, fast and usually the cheapest option. There are many different bus companies, and the lack of a centralised booking system sometimes makes it difficult to find the service you want. At bigger bus stations, the different bus companies each have their own ticket windows. The destinations they serve are normally listed nearby. When you buy a ticket, they'll tell you which bus stop the bus leaves from. Your ticket will be checked when boarding and there is a luggage compartment for bulkier items. Buses are usually air conditioned and have toilets (although, you may have to ask the driver to unlock the door).

The website *www.movelia.es* gives information on many different bus companies, making finding the correct one easier, and allows you to book online. The 'change language' option is at the top left. Movelia charges a small commission for booking tickets, but this is usually worth it because their website makes the whole process much easier. However, you will need to print your tickets.

Tourist Information Offices usually have information about routes and timetables and sometimes also sell tickets.

Many **Travel Agencies** will book bus tickets for a small (5€ or so) commission, however, they often just log on to *www.movelia.es* and do it there.

PLANE

The "low-cost airlines" which have proliferated in Europe recently, use a variety of "tricks" to allow them to advertise extremely low fares which, by the time you've finished booking, mysteriously morph into expensive fares. They do this by charging extra for such items as: using certain credit cards, checking in at the airport rather than online, checking in bags, insurance, priority boarding, taxes, etc. If you play your cards right, you can avoid most of these charges. A website with some useful tips is: *www.tinyurl.com/y8nczrc*

The EU has some strict rules governing what you can and can't carry in hand luggage (carry-on). For general information see *en.wikipedia.org/wiki/Hand_luggage*

The following airlines fly to destinations on or near the Camino from within Europe:

Aer Lingus *www.flyaerlingus.com*	Air Berlin *www.airberlin.com*
Click Air *www.clickair.com*	Easyjet *www.easyjet.com*
Iberia *www.iberia.com*	Ryanair *www.ryanair.com*
Spanair *www.spanair.com*	Vueling *www.vueling.com*
Germanwings *www.germanwings.com*	

If you're flying from further afield *www.skyscanner.com* is a useful website which gives prices either country to country or city to city for many different airlines.

BUS (COACH) TRAVEL AROUND EUROPE

For information about travelling by **bus** around Europe, see the Eurolines website at *www.eurolines.com*.

FERRY TRAVEL TO SPAIN
There are direct ferries from Portsmouth and Plymouth, in England, to Santander and Bilbao. See *www.brittany-ferries.co.uk.*

Camino-related websites
The amount of Camino-related information available on the internet increases every year. Listed below are a few of the most useful in English and Spanish.

IN ENGLISH
Among the most useful and informative sites are the **Camino Forums,** where pilgrims of all levels of experience meet to exchange advice, information and stories. Probably the best for someone who's just starting to learn about the Camino is *www.caminoforums.com.* This site has a friendly and welcoming community of experienced pilgrims who are happy to answer questions. Another good forum can be found at *www.caminodesantiago.me/board*

Both of these forums are quite mature, meaning that all the most common questions have been asked and discussed at length at least once in the past. To get the best from them, it's best to start by taking the time to browse the discussion threads, the more useful ones are *pinned* to the front page to make them more easily accessible, or use the forum's search function to see what you can find. Then, if you still need to, start asking questions.

This link should bring you to real time weather information for the route over the Pyrenees *tinyurl.com/kktr9pc*

The **Canadian Company of Pilgrims** have an excellent website with downloadable guides dealing with subjects such as camping, luxury hotels, etc. They even have a Camino recipe page! *www.santiago.ca*

The **American Pilgrims** site is good too *www.americanpilgrims.com*

Besides running their own pilgrim hostel in Rabanal, the **Confraternity of St James** from the UK, publishes a much respected guide to accommodation, not just for the busy Caminos but also for the neglected ones. They can be ordered from *www.csj.org.uk*

The official website of the archdiocese of Santiago has been developed into a valuable source of information for pilgrims. It's at *peregrinossantiago.es*

The **Pilgrim Roads** website has some interesting interviews with pilgrims *www.pilgrimroads.com*

This website has an interesting English translation of the **Codex Calixtinus** *sites.google.com/site/caminodesantiagoproject/home*

IN SPANISH
One of the best sources of information is from the **Eroski** co-operative group, which provides up-to-date information on pilgrim hostels and everything else you could possibly need to know. They also run a lively discussion forum where pilgrims, can share information and "reviews" of individual hostels *caminodesantiago.consumer.es*

Mundi Camino is another site with loads of information and a shop for Camino souvenirs *www.mundicamino.com.* The **Godalesco** website is another great source of information about all the other Caminos besides the Camino Francés *www.godesalco.com*

The **Jacobeo** website has lots of information, although it's a bit complicated to navigate *www.jacobeo.net.*

The site *www.editorialbuencamino.com* has an excellent interactive maps of all the Camino routes in the Iberian Peninsula.

If you're interested in statistics, the Archdioceses of Santiago compiles records of pilgrims arriving there. Their annual reports can be downloaded from Source: *peregrinossantiago.es/eng/pilgrims-office/statistics*

And finally, this is the website of the **Amigos del Camino**, a voluntary organisation which runs a network of hostels *www.caminosantiago.org*

Budget

You can walk the Camino, staying in pilgrim hostels and eating Pilgrim Menus in restaurants, for about **27€ a day**. That figure is based on the following reckoning:

- **Hostel accommodation**: 3€ to 12€, average 8€.
- **Menú de Peregrino**: 8€ - 12€, average 10€. Three courses with wine and bread, quality very variable, but generally, if you eat meat, it provides enough calories, protein and carbohydrates to keep you going (vitamins are another matter).
- **Breakfast**: 3€, coffee and *bollería / Danish*
- **Lunch and snacks (Bocadillo/Sandwich, Tortilla, Fruit, etc)**: 6€

The biggest expense on the Camino tends to be food and drinks, the prices of which vary a lot from place to place, with cafés and restaurants in cities being considerably more expensive than villages. On the other hand, groceries tend to be cheaper in big urban supermarkets than in small village shops.

HOW MUCH DO OTHER THINGS COST?

Fruit and vegetables vary a lot in price depending on the season and place. The best place to buy is from the local street or covered market (these are the indigenous ancestors of the fashionable urban *Farmers' Market*), where local, seasonable fruit and vegetables should be cheapest. The quality and price in supermarkets is also quite good. In villages, they charge whatever they feel like charging, which can be extremely cheap or extremely expensive.

Bread also varies a lot in price. The best place to buy is straight from the baker's shop or van (they drive around villages blowing their horn and people come out and flag them down). For a standard loaf of white bread, you'll pay between 0,50€ and 1€.

Cheese isn't cheap. For 250g of local cheese expect to pay about 3€ in village shops. It's worth stocking up in urban supermarkets, where it'll be cheaper and there will be a far bigger selection.

Pasta tends to cost between 1€ and 2€ for a 500gr pack, but is cheaper in supermarkets.

Staples of the Spanish diet like **beans**, **lentils**, **chorizo** (sausage) and **rice** tend to be cheap everywhere because it's what the locals eat. There's also a wide variety of canned vegetables, beans and meats (and sometimes combinations of all three in stews and soups) which you can heat and eat.

Toiletries, toothpaste, soap, etc. Tend to be cheaper in supermarkets.

Alcohol, a draft beer (*caña*) costs between 1,10€ and 2,50€, tending to be more expensive in urban areas. Bottled beer is slightly more expensive again. Beer in shops is only slightly cheaper. Wine by the glass varies a lot depending where you are and the type of establishment, 0,50€ to 2,50€ (villages, especially those in wine regions, are cheapest). There is no standard size for a glass of wine. In shops, you can get a cheap (and nasty) bottle for about 1€ and a decent bottle for about 5€. In wine regions, the village shops often sell the local wine in unlabelled bottles. It's what the locals drink so you can't go far wrong. Ask for *El vino del pueblo* or *el vino de aquí*.

Soft drinks (Coke, Aquarius, Fanta, etc.) in cafés usually cost about the same as a draft beer and vary to the same extent. Sold from shops and vending machines, they usually cost about 1€ for a 330ml can.

Cigarettes are still pretty cheap by European standards. A pack of twenty costs about 5€.

REDUCING YOUR COSTS

If you're on a tight budget, here are some ways you can reduce your costs:

Accommodation: Only stay in cheaper hostels. You could probably save about 4€ or 5€ a day by choosing your accommodation merely based on price. In practice, this would mean relying on Municipal, Xunta and Donativo hostels. This works as long as you arrive at your destination early because those are the hostels that fill up first. Another alternative is camping, the pros and cons of which are dealt with under, *What to bring – other equipment,* page 24.

Cooking: Preparing your own meals will save you some money, with the following caveats:

- You'll have to stay in hostels which have a kitchen. With a little forward planning this is fairly easy enough to do, except in Galicia.
- You'll also have to content yourself with the basic selection of groceries available in village shops; typically: pasta, rice, beans, lentils and fruit and veg.
- You're happy to expend the extra time and effort involved in shopping, cooking and cleaning up afterwards (all of which, of course, can be great fun).
- You'll have to eat mostly vegetarian because meat is expensive, and because of the limited cooking facilities (see page 46) and time available. (If you're a meat-eater, and especially if you like a glass of wine, the Pilgrim Menu actually is quite good value for money).
- You're happy to carry some basics like olive oil, pepper, etc.
- Sharing the effort and expense with other pilgrims can make cooking for yourself much easier and cheaper. Lots of pilgrims are happy to get involved in communal cooking adventures. It can be a lot of fun and it's a great way to get to know people better.

Snacks/Lunch: Buying bread and cheese, etc. from the local shop can save you some money. However, the price difference isn't going to be that big when café food tends to be pretty cheap anyway.

RIP-OFFS

The non-commercial nature of the Camino, and the fact that most pilgrims limit their spending to the essentials, apart perhaps from an occasional night in a hotel or a meal in a decent restaurant, means that it has not attracted the kind of commercial hustle or development associated with tourist resorts. At time of writing, it is still possible to walk the Camino Francés without passing a single Starbucks. A happy state of affairs which will surely soon end. Outside of the cities, you're not even likely to see any tourists, and in the cities the tourism is mostly of a high-brow, cultural type.

So **tourist hustles** and **rip-off** artists **are not a major problem** on the Camino, and the likelihood is that your overwhelming experience will be of decent food and drink for reasonable prices, served in a good-humoured, informal manner.

That is not to say that there isn't a certain amount of raising of prices for pilgrims to slightly higher than normal, or even occasionally charging pilgrims more than the locals. However, when it does happen it's mostly on such a modest scale that you're unlikely to even notice.

A good rule in cafés is to ask how much something costs before ordering it. However, cafés are obliged by law to display a **price-list** for all the drinks they sell. If it's easily accessible, you can check first to see how much things should cost. Whether the price-list is prominently displayed or not is sometimes a good indication of the mindset of the owner.

Always having a supply of **loose change** puts you in a stronger position if it comes to a disagreement over how much to pay.

If you're particularly unhappy, ask for the complaints book *libro* or *hoja de reclamaciones*, or go to the Tourist Information and ask for their complaints book. Making a complaint in the *hoja de reclamaciones* will not get you your money back, but it will alert the authorities to the facts of the matter, and leave it up to them to decide if any action against the business is necessary. The mere fact of asking for the complaints book may be sufficient to bring about a change in how you're treated (although there's no guarantee it will be for the better). Restaurants, cafés and other businesses dealing with tourists are legally obliged to have an official complaints book and to give it to you if you ask for it. This is then checked regularly by the authorities and, in theory at least, acted upon. In Galicia, they're also obliged to have a sign displayed saying '*complaints forms are available on request*', or words to that effect, in the local languages and English and French.

Spanish public holidays

Public holidays don't really affect the Camino much. With the exception of pharmacies, banks, post offices and medical centres, everything else tend to open more-or-less as normal. The exceptions are:

- Christmas and New Year: In Spain this period extends from 24 December to 7 January. During this time businesses of all sorts will be working reduced hours and many pilgrim hostels will be closed (see Walking in Winter, page 9)
- San Fermines in Pamplona: Commonly known as *The Running of the Bulls*, from 7 to 14 July. During this time the city is overrun by drunken hordes and the

municipal hostel is closed to pilgrims. The popularity of this festival makes finding affordable accommodation practically impossible. Generally, pilgrims have no choice but to sleep someplace before Pamplona and walk through during the day. This isn't a major inconvenience as long as you plan for it.

NATIONAL PUBLIC HOLIDAYS

1 January Año Nuevo/New Year; **6 January** Día de los tres Reyes/Three Kings; **1 May** Día del Trabajador/Worker's Day; **Easter:** Jueves Santo/Holy Thursday, Viernes Santo/Good Friday; **15 August** Asunción/Ascension; **12 October** Fiesta Nacional/National Holiday (also El Pilar/Día de la Hispanidad); **1 November** Día de todos los Santos/All Saints; **6 December** Día de la Constitución/Constitution Day; **8 December** Inmaculada Concepción/Immaculate Conception; **25 December** Navidad/Christmas.

REGIONAL PUBLIC HOLIDAYS

Navarra Lunes de Pascua/Easter Monday. **La Rioja 9 June** Día de la Rioja/La Rioja Day. **Castilla y León 23 April** Día de Castilla y León/Castile y León Day. **Galicia 25 July** Santiago Apostol/St. James' Day also called Galicia Day.

When a holiday falls on a Sunday, usually another day is given in lieu. However, it may be at a completely different time of the year.

The Credencial / Pilgrim Passport

The *Credencial* (sometimes called a *Pilgrim Passport* in English) is a fold-out piece of paper or booklet, that pilgrims carry to identify themselves as pilgrims. It allows them to use hostels on the Camino intended only for pilgrims on foot, cycling, or on a horse or donkey.

Your *Credencial* will have your name and address and passport number and information such as where you started your Camino and how you're travelling (on foot / by bicycle, etc).

Each hostel will stamp your Credencial and write in the date you stayed there. This is the only evidence accepted in the **Pilgrims' Office** in Santiago that you have fulfilled the necessary conditions to be issued with a *Compostela* (see next section). So keep your *Credencial* safe! If it gets wet, the ink from all those stamps will run and you'll end up with a multi-coloured mess. Which would be a pity because, besides being necessary for claiming a *Compostela*, your *Credencial* also makes a great souvenir of your Camino.

You can get a *Credencial* from the Friends of the Camino association in your home country (see Page 142), or from the Pilgrims' Office in Saint-Jean, or any of the major municipal hostels along the Camino. They usually cost about 4€.

While in the past anyone could issue *Credenciales*, now-a-days the Pilgrims Office in Santiago only accepts those issued by recognised organisations. A full list is on their website *peregrinossantiago.es/eng/preparation/associations-worldwide*

The Compostela

The *Compostela* is the certificate issued by the Pilgrims' Office in Santiago to pilgrims it considers to have completed the pilgrimage in a satisfactory manner. This means, by their definition, that they walked the last 100km of a Camino (it doesn't have to be the Camino Francés) or cycled or rode a horse or donkey for the last 200km. What they walked besides that has no bearing on whether or not they get a Compostela.

The modern *Compostela* is a fairly recent invention and only dates from 1970. However, various kinds of certificates validating the completion of the pilgrimage have been issued by the ecclesiastical authorities in Santiago since the earliest days of the Camino.

You can obtain your *Compostela* from the Pilgrims Office in Santiago. Besides a stamped *Credencial*, you may also be asked for your passport. You'll also be asked to specify why you did the pilgrimage. The answer you give will determine what type of *Compostela* you receive. There are two types:

A **Religious** *Compostela*: you will receive this if you say you completed the pilgrimage for **purely religious** or **religious/spiritual reasons**. It's very ornate and written in Church Latin.

A **Non-Religious** *Compostela* (aka *Certificado*): you will receive this if you say you completed the pilgrimage for any other reason. It's less ornate and written in Spanish.

Camino lore produces the occasional story of the Pilgrims' Office in Santiago subjecting pilgrims' *Credenciales* to very close examination and even refusing people who they judge do not meet the minimum requirements. While these instances do appear to be extremely rare, it's a good idea, if you're only walking the last bit, to get stamps from a couple of cafés along the way every day, as well as whatever hostels you sleep in.

FINISTERRE AND MUXÍA

Walking to Finisterre and Muxía also earns you a certificate.

A **Fisterrana** is like a Compostela but for walking the Camino from Santiago to Finisterre. Issued by the Xunta hostel in Finisterre, it's necessary to have the stamps from various hostels between Santiago and Finisterre to show that you actually walked. It's very flash and in Galician.

A **Muxiana** is like a Fisterrana, but for walking to Muxía from either Santiago or Finisterre. It's available from the Tourist Information Office on the quays, again on production of evidence. If you're walking from Finisterre, it's advisable to get a stamp from the café in Lires, which is about mid-way between the two, as proof that you actually walked the distance. You may be refused a Muxiana, and accommodation in Muxía's over-the-top Xunta hostel, if you don't have the Lires stamp.

ON THE CAMINO

This chapter is intended to give you an idea of what it's like when you're walking the Camino. It starts with a description of a typical Camino day and then moves on to a more detailed description of different aspects of day-to-day life for pilgrims on the Camino.

Most of the time on the Camino Francés, you'll pass through a village with a café, and possibly a shop, about every hour. However, there are some places where you'll walk for up to four hours in open country. Always check the distance to the next inhabited place before setting off, and make sure you have enough food and water to get you there comfortably.

A typical Camino day

The day starts early, probably earlier than you're used to, but don't worry because you'll quickly get used to being up at the crack of dawn. You're awoken about 05:30 by the first movements in the dormitory as the early risers get ready to hit the road. There are whispered conversations and people trying to pack their sleeping bags away without making too much noise. By 06:00 everybody is awake and moving, or at least contemplating moving.

You get yourself out of bed, roll and pack your sleeping bag (you packed everything else the night before), use your torch to check quickly if you've forgotten anything, fill your water-bottle in the hostel kitchen and, within a few minutes, you're outside in the cool morning air greeting other pilgrims, stretching and yawning. There's some low-voiced discussion about options for breakfast and, as the sky turns slowly from black to dark blue, you set off with a small group of other pilgrims in search of coffee and something sweet.

On the village's main street there's a café that's already open. Pilgrims sit around at tables drinking *cafés con leche* or tea, and eating toast or chocolate croissants. You order your coffee and croissant and your group takes an unoccupied table. The television is on, showing the morning news. Nobody pays any attention till the weather comes on, then the café falls silent for the only news that matters from the outside world. The weather looks good, although there's a chance of rain later in the week. So, nothing to worry about.

With the coffee reviving you, you fall into conversation with your fellow pilgrims about the day's walk. Guide books are consulted and compared, and the pros and cons of the different options for tonight's hostel are discussed. A vague plan is formulated, you use the bathroom and you're ready to go. It's about 06:30, you put on your backpack and to a chorus to "*Buen Camino*", you head out. It's bright outside now and down the street you can clearly see the first yellow arrow of the day.

You head off at a good pace. The sky is pale blue and the countryside is flat and open. Up ahead, you can see other pilgrims walking alone or in groups. Your backpack feels a bit heavy today, but every day it feels a bit different. On some days it feels so light you think you forgotten something back at the hostel. Generally, it's comfortable on your back, and after all these days walking you hardly notice it any more.

You pass people walking more slowly than you and, from time to time, you're passed by someone faster. You greet pilgrims with, "*Hola*" or "*Buen Camino*". Sometimes it's just a friendly greeting, and sometimes you talk for a while before one of you pulls ahead. The ground underfoot is hard-packed earth, with quite a lot of small stones. You walk about an hour and a half to the next village, where you pass another café with pilgrims outside drinking coffee in the morning sun.

A friend of yours joins you, and together you continue walking to the next village. By now it's almost 10:00 and you're getting peckish. At a café on the main street you order a *tortilla de patata* and an *Aquarius* (a lemon-flavoured rehydration drink popular with pilgrims) to drink.

You linger for half an hour, talking with other pilgrims. You've covered 13km already and there's another 10km to your destination. The sun is high in the sky now and it's starting to get hot, so you set off, keen to arrive before the heat of the afternoon begins. Solar mid-day in Spain is about 14:00, the hottest part of the day starts then – so it's a good idea to be under cover.

After applying sunscreen to your face and arms, you're off again. You're walking more slowly now because you're starting to tire and because of the heat. You adjust the straps of your backpack to change its position slightly. By the time you arrive at your destination, it's just after 13:00. The hostel is on the mains square with a big sign, *Albergue Municipal*. The French *hospitaleras* check you in and explain the house rules in faltering English. Later, you find out that they're retired primary school teachers.

In the hostel, you get a bed and find you're sharing a dormitory with several people you already know. You unfold your sleeping-bag on your bed, and go outside to do ten minutes of calf and knee stretching, always a good way to relax those calf muscles after a long day's walking and to relieve knee pain. Then you have a shower, put on your other set of clothes and your sandals, use the sink to wash the clothes you wore while walking, and hang them out to dry. Then you set out to see the local sights. This is a typical village of Spain's northern *Meseta*, and your sight-seeing doesn't take long: the tiny church, mud-brick houses (many abandoned and semi-ruined), a few chickens, the village dogs lying in the middle of the road, etc.

In a village café, you find some friends sheltering from the sun and drinking beer. You exchange news about where you've been sleeping, mutual acquaintances, injuries, hardships, encounters, experiences and other typical "Camino talk". Some of your friend go back to the hostel for a siesta, but you stay for another while and end up with a couple of friends, wandering around the village aimlessly, talking about this and that, admiring the local cats and taking some photos.

Later, you run into another friend who says they're planning to cook dinner in the hostel and he invites you to join them. You're happy for a break from the *Menus de Peregrino*, and go with them to the local shop to buy what you need. The shop is a tiny, one-room affair with a glass-fronted aluminium counter stuffed with cured and smoked meats, cheeses and yoghurts, and shelves reaching to the ceiling crammed with every manner of food and other groceries. You buy pasta and vegetables and several bottles of local wine.

Back in the hostel, you scour the kitchen for cooking equipment and other essentials. You find salt and pepper and garlic. The cooking begins with a multi-lingual team of cooks. Soon they serve up a huge pot of pasta and a gang of hungry pilgrims tuck in.

After dinner, with the washing-up done and the kitchen left spick-and-span, there's time for a nightcap in the local café, before, it's back to the hostel to retrieve your laundry from the line and pack you backpack in preparation for an early start. At 21:30 you fall into bed with the dormitory lights still on. Your valuables are safely under your pillow together with your ear-plugs, in case they're needed. This has been your 14th day walking and you're physically exhausted and ready for bed. You're asleep almost immediately.

Walking surface and terrain

SURFACES

The walking surface on the Camino varies from concrete and asphalt to gravel. This is a summary of the most common.

In rural areas the surface you'll be walking on is mostly **earth track** with, in places, quite a lot of **loose stones** (size approx up to 2cm in diameter). This is quite a good walking surface but after a period of dry weather it will get very hard, not quite as hard as concrete but not far off. Also, regardless of the weather, the loose stones can be tough on your feet. In some places on the Meseta the ground turns to sticky mud after rain making it impossible to walk on because you'll quickly have a couple of kilos stuck to each foot. Walking alongside the path is often the only solution.

When passing through urban areas you'll be walking on hard, artificial surfaces: **asphalt, concrete** or **paving stones**. These paved parts are frequent but mostly short – from one end of a village to the other. However, there are several places entering and leaving cities with paved stretches of up to 15km. These surfaces are hard to walk on over long distances. One advantage of them is that they aren't much affected by weather, except for sunlight which they will absorb and radiate heat.

In some parts of the Meseta, where the Camino follows a road, the local authorities have built **walking tracks running parallel to the road**. These have a **hard soil surface** with a coating of **small gravel**. It's not bad for walking on, and it doesn't reflect the heat, has good grip and performs the same in all weathers. If you find walking along the side of a road a bit tedious (especially those long, straight Meseta roads which seem to go on for ever), luckily in most places there's an alternative route which avoids the road. They're signposted and indicated in guide books.

In summary, the Camino Francés is about **72% gravel strewn soil track,** and about **28% various kinds of paved surface**. The **long stretches of paved surface** around seven major urban areas (Pamplona, Logroño, Burgos, León, Astorga, Ponferrada and Santiago), account for **12%** of the total Camino. The other **16%** of paved surfaces is shorter stretches around villages and is spread out along the length of the Camino.

TERRAIN

Long stretches of the Camino Francés are pretty flat, but there are a few places where there are long ascents and descents, the most notable being:

- Saint-Jean to Roncesvalles ascends 1200m and descends almost 500m
- The descent from the highest point on the Camino into El Bierzo is 900m
- Up to O Cebreiro ascends 600m
- From O Cebreiro to Triacastela descends 600m

Leave extra time for ascents and descents, and remember you'll feel more tired after them, especially the first day's climb between Saint-Jean and Roncesvalles, which may take you several days to recover from.

Depending on your level of fitness, steep ascents will probably slow you down quite a lot. If your normal walking speed is 4km/h, on a steep ascent, such as those mentioned above, this could easily drop to 2km/h. Also remember, going downhill can be as difficult, both physically and psychologically, as going uphill.

In a few places, there are climbs and descents where loose stone can make it hard to keep your footing. However, these are rare, generally pretty short, and are passable with care.

None of the mountainous parts are so high or difficult that they require any specialised equipment. However, in bad weather take local advice about when and how to proceed.

Waymarkings / Signposting

The Camino is extremely well waymarked and it's difficult to get lost. Painted **yellow arrows** are the most common form of waymarking. These are regularly maintained by the wonderful volunteers from the *Amigos del Camino / Friends of the Camino*. In most cases these yellow arrows are all you'll need.

That said, in recent years some **towns and cities** have introduced 'official' waymarkings, and obliterated the yellow arrows. In different places, these take the form of:

- Metal scallop-shells or glass plates set into the ground (León).
- Tiles set into the ground (various places).
- Signposts similar to road signs (Burgos).

So, basically, urban areas are a bit of a free-for-all. However, urban waymarkings, with a few exceptions, are generally pretty well thought out. If you do manage to stray you will soon be accosted by complete strangers offering directions, or for non-Spanish speakers, a shove in the right direction.

Alternative routes aren't always particularly well-signposted. The Camino authorities are sometimes over-fond of the notion of there being *one official route*, despite this having no basis in history. One result of this is that some towns with a long history as a pilgrim centre (such as Lugo) don't even come within an ass's roar of the modern *Official Camino*. Another result is that the official waymarkings often give the impression that there is no alternative to walking along the side of a road for tens of kilometres. Luckily, semi- and un-official waymarkings tends to counteract this, and make an effort to point out alternative routes.

Vested interests also play a role in attempting to guide your choice of route. There are occasions where café and hostel owners on one branch of the Camino have engaged in campaigns of ostentatious and exaggerated painting of yellow arrows to try to guide pilgrims in their direction. There have even been cases of them painting over arrows which point in the other direction. These cases of sabotage are usually pretty easy to spot, and shouldn't cause you problems if you are aware in advance of the alternative routes and use your guidebook to see where the Camino divides.

In **Galicia,** there are official waymarkings in the form of concrete posts about 1m high with a scallop-shell symbol on them. It's important to get used to watching out for these if you continue west of Santiago to Finisterre. They are usually angled in the direction you need to follow.

If you're walking west to east (ie. the opposite direction to most people) then watch out for blue arrows. These point towards Saint-Jean.

Weather

The Camino Francés passes through three distinct climate regions. The following descriptions are generalisations. The whole length of the Camino can experience prolonged rain, gale-force winds and cold at any time of the year. But in summer this is much less likely.

Typical weather conditions are described for summer and winter. In the in-between seasons you can get either kind.

Mountainous: on high ground from Saint-Jean to before Pamplona, and again from after Astorga to Molinaseca. In summer, the days are warm and the nights are chilly, and the higher you go the colder it gets. At the highest points the temperature is rarely above 20°C. In winter it can be well below freezing with snow. It can be windy at any time.

Mediterranean: from Pamplona to after Astorga. In summer, generally dry and hot. Typical daytime temperatures are in the low to mid 30s°C. Occasionally up to 40°C. In winter temperatures are normally a little above freezing, persistent rain is not unusual. The flat terrain means it can get quite windy.

Atlantic: Galicia. In an Atlantic climate with westerly winds you can expect rain all year round. The Atlantic winds keep it cool in summer, when it will typically be mid 20s°C, but also mild in winter when temperatures in the mid-teens are not unusual.

WEATHER CHART

Temperatures given are *Average Daily Maximum* and *Minimum*. Precipitation is the average rain or snow fall for the month.

	August			January		
	Max	Min	Precipitation	Max	Min	Precipitation
Roncesvalles	25°C	17°C	8.9cm	12°C	5°C	13.2cm
Pamplona	30°C	16°C	2.3cm	10°C	2°C	2.79cm
Burgos	27°C	12°C	2.4cm	7°C	0°C	4.5cm
León	27°C	12°C	2cm	7°C	0°C	5.5cm
Ponferrada	28°C	14°C	1.7cm	8°C	1°C	5.1cm
Santiago	25°C	13°C	5.1cm	11°C	4°C	20.1cm

Pilgrim hostels / *albergues*

The institution of the pilgrim hostel pre-dates the Camino de Santiago, and dates to the earliest days of Christian pilgrimage to Rome and Jerusalem. In those days, they were usually run by orders of nuns or monks, and were attached to a monastery or a convent. Later, pilgrim hostels were established and run by military orders (such as the *Knights Templar*) or by secular authorities (such as town councils or the nobility), keen to attract pilgrims to their region and to reap the prestige and economic benefits of pilgrimage.

Today, the Caminos leading to Santiago boast a wide variety of pilgrim hostels run along different lines, some as businesses, some by the state or local authorities, and others by religious or secular non-profit organisations.

The main types on the Camino Francés are:

Municipal: run by the local community. They come in all shapes and sizes. Some are fairly basic, whereas others are of recent construction and almost luxurious. They're usual staffed by employees of the *Ayuntamiento* (G), although some of the smaller ones may be staffed by volunteers. The experience of staying in a *Muni* varies hugely depending on its size. The big ones are impersonal, and at times intimidating. The small ones can be cosy and welcoming.

Religious: run by a formal religious community, such as a monastery, or a lay religious community. Most hostels owned by **formal religious communities** are actually run day-to-day by volunteers. They're often quite big and a bit impersonal but sometimes housed in impressive medieval buildings, adding to the sense of history. Those run by **lay communities** are usually smaller and more personal. They're often run by individuals dedicated to bringing the Christian message, in its purest form, into the lives of pilgrims. Religious hostels take all comers, regardless of their religious beliefs. Many also organise a religious service for pilgrims. While some hostels emphasis that attendance is voluntary and everybody is welcome, others are more traditionally Catholic in their approach. Religious hostels are sometimes *donativo* and may organise a communal evening meal, which pilgrims help prepare.

Parish: run by the local church and parish community. These are usually small, welcoming and run by volunteers. Sometimes they include a religious service, and at other times pilgrims are left to their own devices, much as you would be in a Municipal. There's also sometimes a communal evening meal.

Xunta: run by the Galician regional government. Xunta (G) hostels are the Galician equivalent of municipal hostels, which they resemble closely, except that they are always staffed by employees of the Xunta, and most of them (even the newest) have kitchens which don't work. They often occupy disused schools which have been renovated to a very high standard.

Private: run as a business and privately owned. This type of pilgrim hostel is rapidly becoming the most common on the Caminos. The owners range from former pilgrims who genuinely care about what they're doing, to friendly family-run establishments, to people who are just in it for the money. Private hostels are regulated in the same way as hotels and guest houses.

Some hostels are also associated with organisations such as the commercial *Red de Albergues / Network of Hostels,* or the voluntary *Amigos del Camino de Santiago / Friends of the Camino de Santiago*. These organisations represent the hostels' interests, and help with tasks such as the recruitment and training of volunteer hospitaleros. See *www.redalberguessantiago.com*

The range of accommodation along the Camino has expanded so much in the last five years, that it's possible to walk it now staying only in private hostels, or indeed guest houses. That was not the case until recently.

Some people may feel inclined to opt for the comfort and predictability of private hostels, and avoid hostels which are described as basic or religious, thinking that they wouldn't fit in or feel welcome. Rest assured that the small, basic hostels which ask only a donation and organise a communal meal will be some of the most genuinely welcoming places you'll ever visit, and may become the experience by which you define your Camino.

If you chose to stay only in guest houses you'll also miss out on the sense of being part of a community of people who live together and share many experiences (besides just the walk). Much of the real experience of the Camino actually happens when you're not walking.

FACILITIES IN PILGRIM HOSTELS

Pilgrim hostels, with very few exceptions, have communal dormitory accommodation. So you'll be sharing a room with between four and possibly over fifty people. Dorms are usually not segregated by sex. Beds are usually bunks.

The facilities in some of the hostels on the Camino are fairly basic. However, **all hostels have at least the following:**

Beds with mattresses: The vast majority of hostels have beds or bunks. A small number of religious hostels use exercise mats on the floor (the thick kind, so quite comfortable to sleep on). Many hostels also have a supply of blankets, although in cold weather there may not be enough for everyone (See Sleeping Bags, under

What to bring Page 10). Overflow hostels, which are made available when demand exceeds supply, and are usually sports halls, also use exercise mats.

Toilets: Bathroom facilities feature modern flush toilets. They're nearly always separated by sex. They're fairly basic and standard, so you're unlikely to encounter any major surprises. Spain, thankfully, does not suffer from the rash of disappearing toilet-seats so common in certain parts of the world, and standards of hygiene, both in hostels and cafés, are generally good.

Showers with hot water: The freezing shower has been largely consigned to Camino history. If you encounter it at all, it will be due to "technical difficulties". That said, its cousin the lukewarm shower lives on, especially at busy times when water heaters can't keep up with demand. Showers are usually in individual cubicles, but occasionally you'll meet the communal kind. If you do sports or are a veteran of the army or boarding school, this will be nothing new to you. However, people who've had a sheltered upbringing may be in for a bit of a shock. Attitudes towards nudity vary greatly among European nationalities, so expect some people to be less demure that you might think is appropriate (ve vill not mention anybody in particular). Surprisingly, for a traditionally Catholic country, Spain scores quite high on the letting-it-all-hang-out scale, so objecting to immodesty is unlikely to get you anything but bemused looks. Practising looking the other way is really all you can do.

Drinking water: Regardless of whether they have a kitchen, hostels all have running water which is (unless they tell you otherwise) fit for human consumption (see Drinking water, page 72).

A place to wash and dry clothes: Hostels always have someplace to wash clothes by hand. This may be in the sinks in the bathroom, or in a dedicated area (inside or out) for washing clothes. There's also nearly always a clothes line where you can hang your clothes to dry. Many hostels also have washing machines and tumbler dryers. It usually costs between 4€ and 8€ for a wash and dry (usually measured by machine so you can save money by sharing a load with other pilgrims).

In addition to the above, many hostels also have the following:

A kitchen: Many hostels (especially Municipal) have a kitchen that pilgrims can use to prepare food. Kitchens usually have: a **cooker** (although not usually an oven), some **pots and pans**, a few blunt **knives**, a random collection of **cutlery, plates, glasses and cups** and a **fridge,** usually containing decaying vegetables and a bowl of something someone cooked a week before and left there with a note saying "Help yourself!" in several languages (please feel free to dump this!) There's usually also one or more of the following: salt, half a clove of garlic, half a packet of pasta, half a packet of rice. Occasionally, kitchens come equipped with microwave ovens instead of a cooker.

A communal area: Where you can sit and meet other pilgrims, eat, drink wine (hostels generally don't have a problem with people consuming alcohol and some of them sell it), read, etc.

A Pilgrim Book / *Libro del Peregrino*: Where you can write the date, your name and nationality, and anything else that enters your head, or just pass the time reading what other people wrote.

Heating: Is almost universal. This is important if you're walking during the cold months. Some hostels also have fireplaces, and it's generally left up to pilgrims to take care of lighting them (and cleaning up afterwards).

Air conditioning: Only some of the newer private hostels have AC. Nowadays, more and more buildings in Spain are air conditioned, but it's nowhere near as common as some other hot countries (the Spanish traditionally relied on doing as little as possible during the hot part of the day – although this is changing). Old buildings with thick stone walls stay cool even on the hottest days.

WiFi: or more accurately, WLAN, is becoming more common, especially in private hostels. However, most WiFi hotspots along the Camino are in cafés and public squares. In Spanish it's pronounced *weefee.*

Hospitaleras / Hospitaleros

The *hospitalero* (male) / *hospitalera* (female) is the person who runs the pilgrim hostel. The plural for a group of both sexes is *hospitaleros.*

They come in all shapes, sizes and backgrounds. In **Private hostels** they're likely to be the owner, a member of the owner's family or an employee. In **Xunta** hostels, they're likely to be an employee of the local town council. In **Parish** and **Religious hostels,** they're most likely to be a volunteer. In **Municipal hostels,** they could be an employee or a volunteer.

Most volunteer *hospitaleros* are people who walked the Camino and decided they wanted to go back to help to run a pilgrim hostel. There are several organisations which recruit, train and manage volunteer *hospitaleros* (The national confraternities are a good place to start if you're looking for more information; see page 142).

Being a *hospitalero* isn't an easy job. Besides greeting and registering pilgrims, they're also responsible for safety and hygiene in the hostel, and making sure everything is running smoothly. They have to deal with a lot of people. Pilgrims today are a pretty diverse lot, and although the vast majority are well behaved, unfortunately on occasion, there are people who cause problems.

Communicating can be particularly difficult given cultural and linguistic differences. The organisations which manage *hospitaleros* put them in teams with a mix of linguistic skills, which should cover most of the main languages. But even then, problems and misunderstandings do occur.

You can make the lives of the *hospitaleros* easier by being patient, by following instructions and by helping out wherever you can. These volunteers are giving their own time to give back to the Camino, and deserve our respect and gratitude. Professional *hospitaleros* aren't particularly well paid and have to deal with the same issues day-in day-out, and generally do so with good-humour and graciousness. They also deserve our respect and gratitude.

Staying in pilgrim hostels – what's it like?

NB. This section refers to all hostels *except* private ones. Private hostels are dealt with in the next section.

Pilgrim hostels open about **noon** or in the **early afternoon**. Pilgrims who arrive before this time sometimes queue, or leave their backpacks in a line to show who came first. Places are allocated strictly on a first-come-first-served basis. You check in individually; an individual may not check in other people or a whole group. Priority goes to pilgrims on foot, followed by cyclists or pilgrims riding a horse or donkey. Non-walking pilgrims are often not allowed to check in until late afternoon. Pilgrims with a support vehicle are sometimes accommodated, but usually only towards evening, when it can be safely assumed that everybody else has already arrived.

When checking in, you should present your *Credencial*, which the *hospitalero* will stamp and date. You will also sometimes be asked for your passport or identity card. Your details will be written into the registration book. You'll pay in advance, in cash; hostels don't accept other forms of payment. If it's a *donativo* hostel, usually there's a box in reception for donations. The *hospitalero* then usually tells you any important information, they need you to know about the hostel, eg. *your dormitory is on the first floor / is number x, choose your own bed/take bed number y, you can use the kitchen / there is no kitchen, doors locked and lights out at 22:00, location of the nearest shop, please clean up after yourself, availability and cost of using laundry facilities.*

Sometimes, in smaller hostels, especially during off-peak months, the door will be open when you arrive but there may be nobody on reception. In these cases, you take a bed and somebody calls round later to do the administrative stuff. There's usually a sign explaining this.

Unless you're unwell or injured, you can only stay one night.

Specific rules relating to what you can and can't do may also be brought to your attention. These may include:

- **Remove your walking shoes** and leave them in a designated area. This is to reduce the smell and clutter in the dormitories and, when it's raining, to stop pilgrims bringing mud into the hostel. This rule may also be applied to walking sticks.
- Put your **backpack** on the floor rather than on the beds.
- No **eating** in the dormitories.
- No **treating of blisters** on the beds/in the dormitories.

Pilgrims usually unroll their sleeping bag on their bed, to show that it's taken. Some dormitories are cramped, so try not to take up too much space with your belongings. If you arrive early, don't assume other beds around you will be free.

Other pilgrims may be resting, so keep the noise down as much as possible. As a general rule, dorms aren't for socialising. Socialise in the communal area.

Help out in any way you can with keeping the hostel clean and tidy. You're a pilgrim, not a tourist, and in many pilgrim hostels pilgrims are expected to contribute to keeping the hostel clean. In hostels run by volunteers, cleaning is the job of pilgrims. Luckily, the vast majority of pilgrims are aware of this and take their responsibility seriously.

After your shower, mop up the floor of the bathroom, if it's wet. There's nearly always a mop and bucket.

The kitchen is likely to get pretty busy, with several groups of people using the same utensils. Washing pots and pans as you finish with them, rather than after you've finished eating, means other people don't have to wait for you to finish or wash up after you.

Bed time, which is usually 22:00, is the time when the front door of the hostel is locked, and, if you're still not back by that time, tough! Some hostels are stricter about this than others, but the *early to bed early to rise* rule is one that is fairly universally respected among pilgrims (although in summer in Galicia this rule is often not strictly applied).

Many pilgrim hostels also forbid leaving the hostel before 06:00, to discourage people from getting up before about 05:30. This is a reaction to the tendency in recent years of a small minority of pilgrims to want to start walking extremely early, which through alarm clocks, head torches and generally rustling around, was depriving other pilgrims of sleep.

Some pilgrims have problems sleeping because of snoring or the heat in dorms. Personally, I find the first week, when I'm still settling into a rhythm, I sometimes don't sleep so well. After that, I'm so exhausted in the evenings that nothing can keep me awake for long. But, I always put my ear plugs under my pillow before bedding down, just in case. I also find that I sleep better at night (and feel more rested overall) if I don't have a siesta, or limit it to half an hour.

PRIVATE PILGRIM HOSTELS

Private pilgrim hostels operate along similar lines to non-private ones, but they are basically businesses and you're a paying customer so you're not expected to contribute to the upkeep. In addition, the following differences are worth a mention.

The procedure on arrival varies, but generally there will be someone there to greet you, take your money (cash), stamp your *Credencial*, enter you in the register and explain the way the hostel works, and possibly plug their restaurant or offer you some kind of all-inclusive full-board deal.

Lights-out time is often more flexible. Sometimes you can stay up as late as you like. However, unless you're in a town or city there won't be much to do, as Camino villages tend to shut down as soon as the pilgrims are gone to bed.

You can generally stay **as many nights as you like**.

Most private hostels are also happy to take reservations. However, some of them don't bother with reservations because they get enough walk-ins and taking reservations is more trouble than it's worth.

Hotels and guest houses

There's a wide variety of accommodation available along the Camino, ranging from luxurious, historic hotels / *paradores* (G) to family-run guest houses / *hostales* or *hospedajes,* to pilgrim hostels / *albergues.*

Guest houses and one and two-stars hotels are common in Camino towns and villages, and some private pilgrim hostels also rent private rooms. Prices vary greatly. Hotels are categorised from five-star down to one. The number of stars is determined by the size of the rooms, the facilities and services offered, and the standard of comfort. This categorisation is regulated by the state.

In cheaper hotels, breakfast is usually not included in the price. One-star hotels and guest houses start at about 30€ for a basic single room with a shared bathroom. Two- and three-star hotels typically have an *en suite* bathroom and cost between 40€ and 60€ for a single room. Generally, the cheaper the hotel the less noise insulation.

At the other end of the price range, a room in a *parador* can cost several hundred euros. Although sometimes cheaper prices are available on *www.parador.es/en*

Double rooms are typically about a third more expensive than singles.

RESERVING ACCOMMODATION

In some private hostels it's possible to reserve ahead, but in non-private hostels it isn't. Local **Tourist Information Offices** are the best source of information about these as they'll often have up-to-date leaflets with contact details for accommodation in Camino towns (see page 58).

In **France,** reserving ahead is far more common and generally all hostels take reservations. This also applies to the private hostels in Saint-Jean. During peak times, it's a good idea to have your first night's accommodation in Saint-Jean reserved.

Food

NB. For more information about food and eating see the Menu Guide, page 124.

Most Camino villages have at least one small grocery shop where you can buy basic food supplies, such as, fruit and vegetables, pasta, rice, beans, tinned foods, bread, cheese and yoghurt.

In addition, many **cafés** also serve food. The terms *café* and *bar* are used more-or-less interchangeably in Spain (*café* is used throughout in this book for simplicity). Both serve alcohol, hot drinks and usually snacks such as sandwiches, etc. Some also serve hot food. Similarly, something calling itself a **restaurante** may be more-or-less identical to the café next door, with a separate dining area, called **el comedor**. A fancy restaurant, often specialising in regional cuisine, is usually called *un Mesón*.

Mealtimes in Spain are generally: **breakfast** about 08:00, **lunch** between 13:00 and 15:00 and **evening meal** after 21:00.

Hot meals available in restaurants generally fall under one of the following categories:

- **Menú del Día / Lunch Menu**, usually includes a starter, a main course, a dessert and bread. Wine or water is often also included. Coffee is usually extra. Served from about 13:00.

- **Menú del Peregrino / Pilgrim Menu**, usually served from 19:00 so a lot earlier than normal evening meal time in Spain. The Menú del Peregrino is timed for the convenience of pilgrims, who go to bed when most Spanish people are sitting down to eat. It is similar to the menú del día, but often poorer quality.

- **Platos Combinados,** a single plate with a mix of different things. Typically meat, chips, eggs, a small salad, etc., with bread.

The food in restaurants along the Camino varies greatly in quality, and generally never strays much from the standard dishes listed in the Menu Guide. The Camino is not a gourmet culinary experience. Much of the food on offer is pretty basic and most Pilgrim Menus don't extend much beyond chips, meat and a token nod in the vegetable direction. Don't worry - you'll be so hungry you'll eat it anyway. The poor food on the Camino is partly down to Pilgrims' unwillingness to complain and their transient nature (ie. these restaurants aren't expecting you again as a customer any time soon). That said, you will encounter the odd gem.

In common with other southern European countries, what people eat and what restaurants serve is still dominated by local cuisine. The foreign dishes on offer (pasta, pizzas, kebabs, etc.) are all recent arrivals and tends not to be very good.

Spanish cuisine, at its best, is wonderful and you can eat very well and relatively cheaply, especially in towns and cities, if you're willing to be adventurous and shop around. The best advice is generally to *eat where the locals eat*.

During the day, most pilgrims carry a small supply of food to help maintain their energy levels. Fruit is excellent for this because it provides a slow energy release, rather than the abrupt burst from, for example, chocolate. Fruit has the additional benefits of providing liquid and vitamins (which can sometimes be difficult to find on Pilgrim Menus).

Some pilgrims prefer to eat their main meal in the middle of the day and then only a snack in the evening. This has the advantage of allowing them to avail of the generally better quality and greater variety of food in the Menús del Día as opposed to the Menús del Peregrino.

REGIONAL SPECIALITIES

Different regions have different specialities depending on the culture of the area and the raw materials available locally. Watch out for the following:

In Navarra, the traditional dishes are **Bacalao al Ajoarriero** which is salted cod, cut into small pieces and cooked with tomatoes, garlic, onions, peppers and potatoes. Also worth trying is **Alcachofas con Almejas / Artichokes with Clams**. Or the vegetarian **Borraja con Patata / Borage with Potatoes**.

Logroño is the capital of La Rioja, and the centre of a major wine producing region. It also has a strong **Tapas** culture in its city centre cafés. Each café specialises in two or three different kinds of tapa, so shop around until you find something you like. Some regional specialities worth sampling are *patatas a la riojana*, boiled potatoes with chorizo, *chuletillas de cordero al sarmiento* which is lamb cutlets grilled on a barbecue fired by vine branches and not forgetting, *orejas de cordero rebozadas*, sheep's ear in breadcrumbs.

In Santo Domingo de la Calzada, a local speciality is **Ahorcaditos**, sweet almond pastry in the shape of the scallop-shell.

Burgos' pride-and-joy is **Morcilla de Burgos** which is black pudding (a sausage made of pigs' blood) and rice filling.

In Mansilla de la Mulas, the local speciality is **Bacalao al Estilo Mansillés / Cod Mansillés Style**, which, not surprisingly, is cod in a tomato-based sauce.

In León, watch out for **Cecina de León**, a beef sausage with a dark appearance, eaten in thin slices. **Morcilla de León,** a sauce made of pig's blood and onions. **Sopa de Trucha / Trout Soup** is as its name suggests. **Trucha Frita / Fried Trout** is sometimes eaten cold. **Chorizo de León** is considerably spicier than the average chorizo. The city also has a strong **Tapas** culture.

Cocido Maragato is the typical dish of the Maragatería region which begins after Astorga. It contains goat's blood sausage, ½ a chicken, pork, a pig's ear, a pig's trotter, a slice of pig's snout, chorizo, chickpeas, cabbage, potatoes and garlic. The meat is served first, then the chickpeas then a soup. Astorga is also famous for its traditional **cakes** and **chocolate**.

In **El Bierzo** you can try the inauspicious sounding **Botido**. This consists of a pig's stomach stuffed with seasoned bones, tongue, ear, snout and sundry other pig pieces, with chorizo and cabbage, all cured and smoked over a period of five days and served piping hot.

In Galicia, the most famous dish is **Pulpo Galego / Galician Octopus**. This is boiled octopus with paprika, salt and olive oil, usually served on a wooden dish. Melide is a good place to try it. Also in Galicia you may find **Caldo Galego**, which is is an excellent stew made with chicken broth and ham but there is an equally delicious veggie version with chickpeas and various vegetables. **Empanadas** are another Galician speciality, they are pies filled with tuna or chorizo, although there are many different kinds. Some bakeries do a veggie version. **Raxa** (pronounced *raja*) is a Galician dish conatining potatoes and ham which is served in the same metal pot that it's cooked in. **Pimiento de Padrón** is a variety of small green pepper which is commonly served in bars. They're cooked either under a grill or fried in olive oil and severed hot on a metal dish with rock salt.

Tips for vegetarians

Many hostels have kitchens which pilgrims can use, and cooking for yourself is your best bet of getting a balanced diet. The staples of a vegetarian diet are commonly available along the Camino, even in small village shops, simply because they feature strongly in a traditional Spanish diet. **Lentils** *lentejas*, **chickpeas** *garbanzos* (and other beans/peas), **rice** *arroz*, **pasta** *pasta* or *macarrones*, **fresh vegetables** *legumbres* **and fruit** *fruta*, **vegetable oil** *aceite vegetal* and **olive oil** *aceite de oliva*.

There also tends to be a selection of **tinned vegetables and beans**. Packets of **nuts** *frutos secos,* are also common, but are often fried *frito* and salted *salado*. **Bread** *pan* is ubiquitous and cheap, although it's all white (similar to Parisian *baguettes* but shorter and thicker). If you eat **cheese** then that's widely available too.

So, finding the basics of a vegetarian diet isn't that difficult, but will require a bit of extra effort.

Camino shops also stock a good selection of "junk" food: **crisps (potato chips)** *patatas fritas*, **chocolate** *chocolate*, **biscuits (cookies)** *galletas*, etc. Remember, you're going to be burning a lot of extra calories.

Supermarkets in cities and towns will have a better selection of everything, including possibly soy yoghurt and milk and possibly desserts.

If you bring a sealable container of some type (*Tupperware*) you can make bigger portions when you're cooking and have enough for lunch the next day.

EATING OUT

The preceding section about regional specialities may have caused you to abandon all hope of ever walking the Camino, or conjured images of having to survive a month on bread and olive oil. And it's true that there are also some bizarre and antiquated laws which stipulate that every restaurant meal must include some meat.

Well, don't despair. **Queen Sofia of Spain** is rumoured to be a vegetarian (although, officially the house of Bourbon keeps quiet about such a private matter), so awareness about vegetarianism has increased a lot in recent years. Besides that, you're not the first vegetarian to walk the Camino, far from it, and restaurants are used to being asked what on their menu is suitable for veggies. Some of them have even started offering vegetarian options which, anecdotal evidence suggests, are improving in quality. That's not to say that the nightmare scenario of *pasta with cold tomato purée* is entirely extinct!

On **Pilgrim Menus** the starters are often vegetarian and, contrary to what you might expect, often as big as, or bigger than, the main course. Most restaurants will accommodate you if you want to order two starters instead of a main. Salads often have tuna by default, you can ask for it without, *sin atún*.

If you eat eggs you can get a protein hit from the **Tortilla de Patata / Spanish Omelette** with Potatoes which is available from cafés all along the Camino.

Plus if there's nothing else on the menu you can touch, most restaurants can rustle up an omelette *sin carne / without meat*.

Alcohol

WINE / VINO

Each of the Spanish Autonomous Communities has their local wines, and the Camino Francés offers a convenient opportunity to sample some of the best. It passes through the following wine producing regions (in east to west order): **Navarra, La Rioja, León, El Bierzo, Ribeira Sacra, Rías Baixas**.

Spanish wines are identified according to a series of strictly applied rules which classify them by region of origin, quality and age. A nodding acquaintance with these rules will help to steer you through the bewildering array of bottles you'll encounter in any decent Spanish supermarket (in villages shops you're only likely to encounter the major brands and the local stuff, often sold in unlabelled bottles).

There are two main **region of origin** classifications:

VINO DE CALIDAD PRODUCIDO EN REGIÓN DETERMINADA / QUALITY WINE PRODUCED IN A SPECIFIC REGION

The region of production and category of the wine will be clearly indicated on the bottle. Regions are ranked (somewhat arbitrarily) according to the quality of the wine they produce:

- **Vino de Calidad con Indicación Geográfica**: the lowest quality.
- **Denominación de Origen**: most regions fall into this category.
- **Denominación de Origen Calificada**: regions with a track-record of producing quality wines, currently La Rioja and Priorat (in Catalonia).

There is an additional category for the highest quality wines, which is applied to individual estates rather than whole regions, **Denominación de Origen de Pago**. Currently, there are only nine estates with this status, six in Castile-La Mancha and three in Navarra.

VINO DE MESA / TABLE WINE

Poor quality (but correspondingly cheap and usually drinkable) wine produced from a mixture of grapes from different regions. **Vino de la Tierra / Local Wine** is similar but may be associated with a specific region.

CLASSIFICATION BY AGE

Additionally, quality wines are classified by age: **Joven** or **Sin Crianza** is the youngest type, having spent less than a year ageing (in La Rioja this type of wine is sometimes called simply Rioja); **Crianza** is aged for at least two years, one of which must be in oak barrels; **Reserva** is aged for at least three years; **Gran Reserva** is aged for at least two years in oak barrels and three years in the bottle.

In La Rioja, the classification by age is indicated by a small coloured label on the rear of the bottle, called the **Consejo**, which also bears the word Crianza, Reserva, etc.

BEER / CERVEZA

Spain is one of those blessed places which, as well as producing wine of outstanding quality, also produces extremely drinkable beers. All the main varieties are **lager** (also known as **Pilsner** or **Blonde**) beers. The most common ones along the Camino are:

- **Mahou** (brewed by Grupo Mahou-San Miguel in Madrid) comes in a variety of flavours, **Cinco Estrellas** is standard, whereas **Clásico** is a US-style light beer.
- **Cruzcampo** (brewed by Heineken International in Seville) is Spain's biggest-selling beer. Its distinctive symbol is the happy-looking Gambrinus, the legendary Flemish king, clutching a glass of his favourite tipple.
- **Estrella Galicia** (produced by Hijos de Rivera, an independent brewery based in A Coruña) is the most common beer in Galicia.
- **Ambar** an excellent beer from Aragon, is also sometimes available.

The local beers compare very favourable to the international brands, which are becoming increasingly common, such as **Heineken** and **Amstel** (also brewed by Heineken International). Cafés generally only have one beer on draft, but usually have a few other brands in bottles in a fridge under the counter. Bottles are usually a little bit more expensive than draft.

There are also many alcohol-free beers which are widely available. The major brands all have a 0% alcohol version, usually called *sin* (*without*), or *0,0%*. They taste as good as the "real thing".

CIDER / SIDRA

There is a long history of **apple cider** production in northern Spain, especially in Asturias, Galicia and the Basque Country. Spanish cider is generally dryer than cider in the British Isles, but less bitter than German Apfelwein.

Asturian cider has a **Denominación de Origen,** and is made exclusively from locally grown apples. Other ciders may be made from a mix of locally grown apples and imported apple concentrate. Cider is served in many cafés, however establishments specialising in it are called **Sidrerías.** They usually also serve food as cider is usually drunk as an accompaniment to a meal.

Bottled Spanish cider is not artificially carbonated, and in order to bring out its flavour it is oxygenated by pouring it from a height of about 1.5m into a shallow glass. In cider drinking regions this is considered the job of the waiting staff, however, outside of those regions, cafés and restaurants are sometimes equipped with a machine which can do it for you (without spilling half of it).

Traditional festivals

Almost every village and town has a traditional **festival** or *fiesta*. Some are famous, like the **San Fermin** in **Pamplona,** but most are known and loved only by the locals. They're often based around the local Saint's day and usually involve a religious element, to justify the massive quantities of eating, drinking, dancing, singing and chasing, and being chased by, bulls.

Some of the bigger ones are worth avoiding, unless you want hordes of people and all-night drinking. Pamplona's being a prime example. Others are local affairs which have, due largely to their obscurity and the efforts of the local community, managed to hold on to what defines them in place and in history. Watch out for them, they're well worth experiencing.

St James' Day is the occasion of a major shindig in Santiago. Opinions among pilgrims are divided about whether arriving into Santiago at that time is a good thing or not. Santiago during the St James' Day week is going to be very crowded, with processions, dignitaries and outdoor events of all descriptions. If you'd prefer a quieter end to your Camino then St James' Day is probably worth avoiding.

Environment

The state of the environment on certain stretches of the Camino Francés can be quite grim, due to industrial and agricultural development, road building, electricity pylons and the general detritus of a modern society. The situation is made worse by the attitude of some pilgrims (a small minority), who just dump their litter wherever they feel like it. This isn't helped by the apparent inability of the civil authorities to empty what few dustbins there are.

The litter situation would doubtlessly be a lot worse if it wasn't for the efforts of voluntary organisations like the *Amigos del Camino / Friends of the Camino* who, besides running many beautiful pilgrim hostels, organise clean-up days along the Camino to pick up the rubbish that other people leave behind.

Your number one contribution to this effort is to dispose of your own litter in the bins provided, even if that means carrying it for a while. Another way you can help is by occasionally picking up other people's litter and putting it in a bin.

Toilets

Many stretches of the Camino are devoid of toilets for many kilometres, so people relieve themselves behind any available bush. In summer, when there are a lot of pilgrims, areas of bushes and trees adjacent to the Camino can become pretty smelly. You can help by, first of all, using toilets whenever possible, and cafés generally don't enforce any 'customers only' policies. However, please bear in mind the following suggestions if you need to relieve yourself in the open:

- Move a little away from the Camino, two minutes walk is plenty. Spreading it out makes it less damaging and less intrusive.
- Carry a plastic bag and put your used toilet paper, etc. in it and dispose of it properly when you get a chance.
- Don't go to the toilet in the vicinity of buildings (it's good manners, if nothing else).

Opening hours

Generally in Spain, everything opens late and stays open late. **Shops** and other businesses, such as **banks,** usually open from 09:00 until 12:00 and again from 17:00 until 20:00, to accommodate the traditional siesta. Shops are also usually closed, or have greatly reduced opening times, on **Sunday** and **Monday**. Banks are closed on **Saturday** and **Sunday**.

However, businesses along the Camino have adapted to the strange hours pilgrims keep, and it's common to see cafés and shops open at 06:00 in the morning, and shops remain open all day (at least in summer). Restaurants serve Pilgrim Menus from about 19:00, much earlier than the normal Spanish evening meal time, 21:00.

Also, as a general rule, the bigger the town, the longer the opening hours.

One source of frustration for pilgrims is the tendency in rural communities for the local **church** to be locked at all times except for religious services, which sometimes only happen once a week. Thankfully, the tourism authorities have taken note and, during the summer at least, communities are being actively encouraged to open their churches for (at least) a few hours a day. Navarra is particularly active in this regard and has produced a leaflet which you can pick up in Tourist Information Offices showing the opening times of the various Camino churches.

Banking and Money

On the Camino, cash is king. Pilgrim hostels do not accept cards of any description. The same is true for shops and cafés. The only safe assumption is that you will have to pay for everything with cash.

Most of Spain's banks are bankrupt and kept alive by an unlimited line of credit from the **European Central Bank**, and various other mechanisms. Despite this, from a visitor's point-of-view, the system continues to function as normal, with an extensive network of **ATMs** (Spanish *cajeros automáticos*) in **towns and cities**. In villages you generally will not find ATMs. Always make sure you have enough cash to cover your needs for a couple of days, or at least until you get to the next town where you know there's a bank.

ATMs generally dispense 20€ and 50€ notes. Bank notes bigger than 20€ are difficult to cash outside of towns. So if the ATM gives you 50€ notes try to spend them in a supermarket or some other urban business which is sure to have change. If you have anything bigger than a 50€, get rid of it as soon as possible.

Sometimes hostels have vending machines for hot and cold drinks and basic groceries. There mightn't always be someone who can give you change, so having a small emergency reserve of coins is a good idea.

If you need someone to send you money in an emergency **Western Union** operate together with the Spanish **Post Office** *Correos*, so you can pick up cash at any Post Office in Spain.

Travellers Cheques are a thing of the past.

For **exchange rates** see *www.xe.com*.

SECURITY

Banks monitor their customers' ATM and credit cards transactions in order to try and identify fraud (stolen or cloned cards). Transactions suddenly appearing from rural Spain may set off an alarm in your bank's computer system, causing it to block your card. The bank may then call you on your home phone and, if there's nobody there to answer, your card remains blocked. For this reason it's essential to be aware of your bank's policies in this regard, some banks ask that you inform them before you travel. If in doubt it's probably a good idea to ask. In addition, you should make a note of a customer service number at your bank, you can call from abroad (freephone and other non-terrestrial phone numbers may not be accessible from outside your home country).

Number formats

Spain uses the euro, the symbol for which is €. In Spain it's written after the amount - 1€ - although you will sometimes see it written before the amount (€1, etc.). Numbers are written using a point as the thousand separator and a comma as the decimal separator, 1.243,12€ (the opposite of what's normal in English speaking countries). Occasionally, an apostrophe is used as the decimal separator, 2'25€. Or the euro symbol is used as the decimal separator, 2€25. Just to confuse things further, prices are also sometimes written without the € sign and minus trailing zeros: 4,5 or 4'5 = 4,50€. This confusion reflects the fact that there is no official standard for how to write euro amounts.

The English plural of euro is *euro* or *euros*, according to one's personal preference. The same applies to cent and cents. They are always written lower-case, unless at the beginning of a sentence.

Tourist Information Offices

Towns and cities usually have a Tourist Information Office on or near the Camino route. They'll usually be able to give you a list of guest houses and hotels on or near the Camino with contact information and in indication of prices.

The Camino in Spain passes through four regions (*Comunidades Autónomas*). Each region has a tourist office on or near the Camino shortly after you cross the border: **Navarra** in **Roncesvalles**, **La Rioja** in **Logroño**, **Castilla-y-León** in **Redecilla del Camino** and **Galicia** in **O Cebreiro**. These can often provide information about the Camino specifically aimed at pilgrims. They usually also have lists of alternative accommodation (hotels, etc.).

Keeping in touch

MOBILE PHONES AND SIM CARDS

The entire Camino is covered by Spain's various **mobile phone networks**. You should check with your home network to see if you'll be able to use your phone in Spain and how much it will cost (if you're from outside the EU it will probably be extremely expensive).

If you will need to make frequent calls while in Spain, or wish to have mobile internet access, then a cheaper option is to buy a Spanish SIM card. The advantages of this are **no roaming charges** for incoming calls and **cheaper calls within Spain** and **internationally**. To be able to use another SIM card in your phone, it must be SIM and network unlocked. Contact your home network about this, they can sometimes supply an unlock code. Failing that, many independent phone retailers also unlock phones (although, this is illegal in certain countries).

You can get an idea of the SIM deals available by looking at sites like *www.spainsim.com* or *www.0044.co.uk/spain.htm*. These sites will ship a Spanish SIM card to you. However, it is also possible to buy a SIM card in Spain. For making international calls **Lebara Mobile** is probably the best option. They offer cheap international calls and data packages. See their website for up-to-date rates *www.lebara-mobile.es* (switch to English in the top right corner).

SIMs cards can be bought from call shops (*Locutorios*). The first ones you'll encounter on the Camino Francés are in **Pamplona**. The legal requirement to register the ownership of pre-paid SIM cards has been relaxed, so no ID or online registration is required when buying one.

Top-ups for prepaid SIMs are widely available in cities and towns. The system for topping up maybe be different from your home country. When you ask for credit you'll be asked for your mobile number (it might be easiest to have this written down), which the shop assistant will enter on their terminal, together with the top-up amount. You will then receive a text message confirming your top-up.

CALLING IN SPAIN

Payphones are already a rarity, and from 2017 if the government gets its way, they will disappear completely. If you find one that works, they take various pre-paid cards, which you can buy in grocery shops, newsagents and Post Offices, or they may also take coins.

In larger towns there are call shops called ***Locutorios,*** where you can call and pay afterwards.

Spanish dialling tones are:

Ringing = a long, steady tone repeated at regular intervals.

Engaged / busy = short tones repeated rapidly.

TO CALL WITHIN SPAIN

Spain has no area / zone codes so you always dial the whole number. Fixed line numbers begin with a **9** and mobiles with a **6**. They always have **nine digits** and are written in groups of three, eg: **912 345 678**. Other numbers, such as freephone, premium, etc. begin with other digits.

TO CALL ANOTHER COUNTRY FROM SPAIN DIAL:

The international access code is **00** (as it is throughout the EU). It is often represented by the + symbol.

00 [country code] [area code minus first digit] [local number].
So if you're calling a number in the US: 212-555-1234 from Spain you would dial 00-1-212-555-1234.

TO CALL SPAIN FROM ANOTHER COUNTRY

The international dialling code for **Spain is 34**. For **France it is 33**. If you're calling from outside Spain, contrary to the practice in countries where phone numbers begin with 0 or 1, you should also dial all digits.

To call **912 345 678** dial **+34 912 345 678**.

INTERNET ACCESS

Internet access is becoming more and more widely available on the Camino. Many cafés and hostels now offer **WiFi,** and some towns and cities even have free access on their main square. Watch out for the WiFi symbol. Usually you'll have to ask for the network key or password *(llave* or *contraseña)*, or it will be written up somewhere. Unfortunately, Skype rarely works on Spanish WiFi.

One consequence of WiFi proliferation and cheaper broadband is that **Internet Cafés** have become an endangered species. **Public libraries** (Spanish *bibliotecas*) in larger town often provide free internet access to the public. You can usually also print there.

Another consequence of WiFi proliferation is that it's harder to disconnect from your real life. Most people go on the Camino to experience something new and different.

A few years ago I met a girl whose primary goal, whenever she arrived into a village, was to find WiFi. I once whiled away a wet afternoon with her and a group of other pilgrims, in a café, drinking wine and talking. The whole time she was on her mobile doing "social media" things. "Social media" on the Camino is a misnomer. It should really be called "anti-social media". How can you really experience the here-and-now when your main preoccupation is who commented on your status update? I actually started avoiding her. Not because I disliked her, but because the Camino for me is an escape from the internet, and a chance to ignore all of that stuff for a few weeks a year.

INTERNET SECURITY

There haven't been any reports of problems along the Camino (it seems to happen more in Madrid), but the danger of having your email account hijacked is something you should always be aware of. Follow the advice of your email provider regarding security. For example, Google's **Gmail** recommend you register a mobile phone number with them, so they can confirm your identity by text message if necessary.

Setting up a **rogue WiFi network** is very easy using an Android mobile phone (though it's possible to do it on other systems too). This can be set up to redirect page requests to fake sites, so when you type *www.gmail.com* or *www.hotmail.com*, your browser opens a page that looks like the real thing but is actually fake, and then takes a note of the user name and password you enter. So, be careful what networks you connect to and avoid *open* networks unless you know who they belong to.

Probably the safest and cheapest way to access the internet while on the Camino is to buy a local SIM card and access it directly from your mobile or other device, over the phone network.

If you do use public computers, be careful to log out everything you logged into. This will delete your credentials from the computer. Just closing the browser without first logging out will not.

POST OFFICES

Most bigger towns have a Post Office. They're usually open Monday to Friday mornings and afternoons. They're yellow with the word *Correos*. Letterboxes are also yellow.

Electricity

Spanish electricity runs on 230V. The type of electrical socket used is the standard *Europlug*. This is used in most continental European countries (with some small national variations). See *en.wikipedia.org/wiki/Europlug*

230V is compatible with UK appliances, although you will need an adaptor.

If you're coming from further afield (for instance, North America), you may need an adaptor / voltage converter, to convert both the socket type and voltage.

If you just need a standard USB charger (such as those used by most recently built mobile phones), it might be cheaper and lighter to buy a Europlug format charger, rather than a converter for your current one.

Health

Spain has an excellent, modern health care system. Health care in the public system is free for Spanish citizens and residents. Citizens of other EU counties must have a current **European Health Insurance Card** (EHIC, formerly E111) to receive treatment in the public system. This must be obtained in your home country.

There is also a private system offering basically the same service in plusher offices with a cute receptionist. If you buy travel insurance which covers medical emergencies, you will probably be directed to the private system.

Towns, and sometimes also villages, have **Health Centres** called *Centro de Salud* or *Centro de Atención Primaria*, where you can see a doctor. You'll have to fill in a form, and possibly they'll ask you to come back at a specific time. Often in villages they're only open a few hours a day or a couple of days a week.

If you are not an EU citizen, it's important to buy some form of **health insurance** which covers medical emergencies and repatriation to your home country. The cost of treatment, even for minor ailments, can quickly become extremely expensive. In the event of your needing emergency repatriation, the costs can easily run into thousands of dollars/euros.

Even if you are an EU citizen, some kind of medical emergency cover is probably also a good idea as the EHIC doesn't cover repatriation in the event of an accident.

Some insurance companies regarding hiking as a dangerous activity and do not cover it in their policies. Check the fine print carefully.

Pharmacies can be found fairly frequently in towns and bigger villages. They're identified by a sign with a green cross on a white background and they usually have opening times similar to other shops.

If you need medical help on the Camino the first place to ask is in a pilgrim hostel. They usually know who to call or where to go.

LOOKING AFTER YOUR OWN HEALTH

There's nothing particularly hazardous about walking the Camino de Santiago. The most common pilgrims complaints are the effects of **overexertion, exhaustion** and **heat.** The most common pilgrim ailments are listed below, with a few tips on how to avoid them (most of them are easily avoided). And failing that how to recognise them and deal with them.

It can't be emphasised too much that **the best strategy is prevention.** Often, this is as simple as planning for these possibilities before setting off, deciding your walking pace for yourself rather than trying to walk at someone else's pace, being flexible and accepting your limits, checking your feet at the first whisper of a blister, paying heed to minor aches and pains and taking action to treat them and prevent them getting worse. And generally exercising common sense.

Serious injury and death are rare, but when they do occur they're usually related to one of the following:

- **Heart attack:** probably the most common cause of death on the Camino. Going up hills is when your heart will be working hardest, so you can reduce the chances of a heart attack by taking hills slowly.
- **Hit by a motor vehicle:** the Camino often crosses busy roads (although, in the past five years most of the dangerous crossings have been replaced with pedestrian tunnels or bridges). Be extra vigilant and always walk along roads facing oncoming traffic (on the left).
- **Exposure (as in to cold):** a rare occurrence but worth mentioning. One pilgrim died of exposure in the Pyrenees in winter 2013. Several other groups got into trouble and had to be rescued. Winter 2013 was unusually harsh and the hills around Roncesvalles were covered in deep snow until mid-May. The Pilgrim's Office in Saint-Jean will tell you if it's safe to walk the Route Napoleon (the higher route over the Pyrenees) or not – follow their advice!

PRESCRIPTION MEDICINE

If you will need to take prescription medicine during your Camino there is a number of points you'll need to bear in mind:

- **Supply:** calculate how much medicine you'll need, get it in good time and make sure the use by date covers the duration of of the trip.
- **Storage:** many medicines need to be stored within a certain temperature range, for this reason (and because of the danger of theft) carry them with you in your hand luggage, rather than checking them in. The temperature in your backpack during periods of extreme weather may also damage medicines. Find out in advance about your medicine's tolerance to extremes of temperature (it usually says it on the packet).
- **Legal issues:** some medicines are not legal in all countries. Ask advice from your pharmacist or doctor. Keep all medicine in its original packaging together with the receipt from your pharmacy or a copy of the prescription. This makes it easier to prove the drugs actually belong to you.
- **Prescription:** if you lose your prescription medicine during the trip it is usually possible to get a replacement locally. This will be greatly facilitated if you have a copy of the prescription and / or a note from your doctor. The replacement medicine may have a different brand name to what you usually get. It may also come in different dosage sizes, so have a record of exact quantity you need (ie. in milligrams). The more detailed information you have about the exact composition of any medicines you need (such as a hard or soft copy of the list of ingredients) the better.

COMMON CAMINO AILMENTS

The one sure way to avoid injury from walking is to take your time, walk at your own pace not somebody else's, and don't try to walk further than you're able to comfortably. Most importantly, listen to the warning signs from your body (pain and discomfort) and heed them!

DEHYDRATION

Dehydration is a danger, especially in **hot weather,** when you should make sure to get at least three litres of (non-alcoholic) liquid a day. Your salt consumption will also affect your level of water retention. Remember, when walking in hot weather you'll need more salt than usual because you'll be losing so much of it through sweating.

As a general rule, drink more liquids than you think you need. Dehydrating caffeinated drinks should be avoided (coffee, cola, etc.), as should alcohol. The symptoms of dehydration are headache, fatigue, discomfort, disorientation and painful joints. A dehydrated person needs to be given lots of water to drink.

SUNBURN, HEATSTROKE / SUNSTROKE

In summer, the heat and sun are the biggest dangers. In western Spain the summer sun is at its highest point shortly after 14:00. The hottest part of the day, and the period during which the sun is strongest, begins then.

Sunburn is caused by exposure to **ultraviolet (UV) radiation**. The higher the sun is in the sky and the less cloud cover, the more UV radiation reaches you. The best protection against sunburn is to minimise your exposure to direct sunlight and use a high-factor sunscreen cream (sun protection factor 20 or above, see below). Pay special attention to the left side of your body because that's where the sun will hit you when you're walking, and to delicate places like ears and the backs of your knees. Follow the instructions for your brand of sunscreen, and remember, its effectiveness is affected by factors such as sweat, dust, etc. Sunburn can be treated by submersion in cool water. For severe sunburn with blistering, medical advice should be sought.

Sun protection factor (SPF) is the amount of ultraviolet radiation required to cause sunburn on skin through sunscreen, as a multiple of the amount required without sunscreen. So with factor 20 on, you need 20 times as much UV radiation to burn you as you would with no protection.

HEATSTROKE (OR HYPERTHERMIA)
Heatstroke is when a person's body temperature goes above 40°C. **Confusion** and **lack of sweating,** are typical symptoms. You can protect yourself from heatstroke by wearing a wide-brimmed, light coloured hat, with ventilation holes, and not exerting yourself on hot afternoons. Affected persons must be cooled as soon as possible. If no cool place is immediately available, they should be sat upright in the shade and given water to drink.

BLISTERS
A blister is a reaction of your skin to friction. They are likely to occur where your skin comes into contact with your boots. They are pockets of fluid within the upper layer of skin, which are intended to protect the skin below from damage. Blisters normally fill with a **clear** (as in transparent) **liquid**. If you have a blister that fills with a **liquid that isn't clear**, you should seek medical advice. The skin below a blister will naturally harden as a reaction to the friction which caused the blister, making it more friction resistant in future. However, getting to that point may be an uncomfortable experience.

Among the pilgrim community blisters is a heated topic. As a consequence, there is a massive amount of advice available around the internet on this subject, much of it contradictory. Strategies for avoiding blisters and the best boots and socks to buy, provoke prolonged and heated debates, in which everybody advocates what worked for them.

The truth is, there is no guaranteed way to avoid blisters, and even experienced pilgrims aren't immune to them. All you can do is minimise the risks and deal with blisters early and appropriately.

The following tips should help you keep your blisters manageable.

BEFORE YOU GO:
• **Buy your boots as early as possible** (at least **six months** before you start your Camino) **and wear them enough to break them in thoroughly,** including on long hikes, in as wide a variety of temperatures and weather conditions as possible, as well as daily wear – even if it's just around the house. You should be able to walk any distance in a broken-in pair of boots and not get blisters or pain in your feet. During the breaking-in process, experiment with your boots. Lace them tightly, lace them loosely, lace them looser at the bottom and tighter at the top, etc. Wear your boots with different kinds of socks, to see what combination works best. Try them with different insoles, or possibly no insoles. If you develop hard, dry skin on your feet's vulnerable edges, all the better. This is the

best defence against blisters. If the breaking-in process doesn't go well, consider changing your boots for something more suitable. **If you don't have six months to prepare** (or even six days), consider your options carefully. The chances are you already own a pair of broken-in shoes you could walk the Camino in. That might be preferable to taking a chance on a new pair of boots, and if it doesn't work out, larger Camino towns and cities all have outdoor shops where you can buy boots (with on-hand expert advice from your fellow pilgrims).

ON THE CAMINO:

- **Treat problems early don't ignore them!** Symptoms of a developing blister include **redness, tenderness** and a **sensation of heat.** Apply plasters (Band Aids, or some kind of sticky medical tape) to friction points **before a blister develops**. A specialised blister plaster called **Compeed** is widely available from Camino pharmacies. Read the instructions! Masking or gaffer tape can also be useful, especially when combined with plasters. Vaseline, or some other lubricant can be helpful on some friction points, such as between your toes. However, lubricating the skin will prevent it becoming dry and hard and immune to blisters, so this strategy must be applied with caution.

- **Take your boots and socks off** whenever you take a break, to let your feet dry and cool. You could also change to a fresh pair of socks in the middle of your walking day. Having **damp/moist** feet increases the likelihood of getting blisters.

- Allow your feet to develop **hard skin** in the places prone to blisters. This is your best protection against more blisters. The things which will prevent this hard skin developing are, prolonged **soaking** in water, applying **moisturising cream**, etc. Some people claim **rubbing alcohol** actually speeds the development of hard skin by drying it out.

- An alternative approach to the previous point, which some pilgrims swear by, is to keep your feet **lavishly moisturised** at all times with some kind of moisturising lotion. This prevents your skin drying and cuts down on the amount of friction between your feet and your boots. That these two approaches completely contradict each other, but work equally well for different people, really proves that there is no one-size-fits-all solution to this problem. And the earlier you start finding out what works for you, the better!

- Don't **shower** in the morning. On the Camino nobody showers in the morning. You shower when you finish walking.

- Alternate **boots** and **sandals** (or any other kind of footwear), during your walking day, and after you finish walking for the day.

- Wear **two pairs of light socks** (or Sock Liners). This reduces friction between your feet and your boots.

- Resist the temptation to soak your feet in lovely cold streams or ponds during your walking day. This will increase your risk of getting blisters.

Because finding out what works for you will involve a certain amount of (possibly painful) trail and error, getting that over with before you arrive on the Camino is your best strategy.

Under **ideal conditions,** this is **how to treat a blister:** Disinfect the skin on and around the blister and, with a sterile syringe, pierce the blister's top end and drain the liquid (it's important that you leave the skin over the blister intact). Then, using another sterile syringe, pump the blister full of disinfectant and allow it a couple of minutes to do its thing. (BTW, that part is pretty painful). Then drain the disinfectant and pierce the blister at it bottom end. Using a sewing needle and surgical string (the type they use for stitching wounds), get a length of string in one hole and out the other. Knot both ends of the string to keep it in place. The string will keep the holes open and prevent the blister refilling. Now protect the blister with some kind of padded bandage. Change the bandage every day until the blister has dried and healed. When not walking, leave the blister exposed to help it heal.

Now, in real life you won't be **operating under ideal conditions,** and you're unlikely to have such an impressive array of medical supplies. However, a more simplified version of the technique described above can be applied under normal conditions and with basic tools. The minimum you need is soap, hot water, something to pierce the blister (this isn't so hard since it's just the outer layer of skin, the nerves are underneath), sterile bandages and a steady hand.

Clean the area, pop your blister (these can blow with quite a lot of pressure so you'd be best to angle it away from yourself, and anyone else in the vicinity), drain it well and clean it (fresh tissue handy here), and apply a bandage or Compeed. If you do this in the evening before you go to bed (depending on your sleeping arrangements), you can leave the blister exposed to the air over-night, to allow it to dry out. But it's important that you bandage it well, or put Compeed on it, before putting your shoes on.

This advice is suitable for treating non-serious cases of blisters. If your blisters have taken on monstrous proportions and are out of control, seek professional medical advice. Also, it's very important, at the first sign of infection, or if the basic first aid described above doesn't work, that you seek professional medical advice.

If you have blisters on the Camino you will probably be the recipient of a lot of contradictory advice and offers of help. There are even *hospiteleros* who specialise in "curing blisters". Don't let anybody treat your blisters unless they're a trained medical professional.

Veteran pilgrims aren't immune to the scourge of blisters, and I'm no exception. I tend to get one blister per Camino, usually about two weeks in, and always on a different part of my foot, but the most likely spots are the outside of my little toe or underneath my big toe. Generally I follow the abbreviated procedure above, pop it in the evening and then keep it bandaged during the day, checking it regularly to make sure it hasn't turned green, until the skin is dry and hard, which usually takes a couple of days. My blisters have never caused me anything more than minor discomfort.

BEDBUGS (LATIN *CIMEX LECTULARIUM*, SPANISH *CHINCHES*)

Bedbugs are insects which live by sucking the blood of humans and other mammals. They became a rarity during the 20th century due to the widespread use of pesticides. However, in recent years they have developed immunity to many pesticides, and the frequency of infestations is increasing, with some US cities particularly badly affected.

Bedbugs are mostly nocturnal and are most active shortly before dawn. They will nest and breed any place dry and sheltered from light. Once established in a building, they are very difficult to eradicate.

They are not believed to transmit disease, and so are more an annoyance than a health hazard. Symptoms of having been bitten are local irritation and inflammation of the skin around the bite, and often multiple bites in clusters or lines. Irritation can last several days but responds well to oral and cream antihistamines.

If you suspect you have been bitten, it's important to thoroughly check your clothes, sleeping bag, backpack, etc. to make sure you're not carrying any bedbugs with you, and to prevent the infestation moving from one hostel to another (not to mention the hassle and expense of infesting your own home). It's also important to tell the *hospitaleros* in which hostel you think you got bitten, so that they can report the problem.

Mature bedbugs are 3mm to 4mm in length, and will usually be found hidden in seams or pockets of clothing or sleeping bags or anything else that provides convenient hiding places. Fortunately, because they're easy enough to spot, **ridding yourself of them isn't that difficult**.

Find a flat open area, preferably in direct sunlight with a light-coloured flat surface. Empty the contents of your backpack to one side and then thoroughly, one item at a time, inspect everything. Open every pocket, every toiletries bag, every zippy bag and check each individual item before putting it on the "checked" side. The things to check most carefully are clothing, sleeping bag and backpack. Turn them all inside out, turn out all of the pockets, inspect every nook and cranny (having light-coloured clothes is an advantage here), and then give it a good shake, before putting it on the "checked" side.

Bedbugs are pretty hardy critters and can apparently survive for up to a year without feeding, although this would depend on them entering a semi-hibernative state. Up to five months between feeds would be fairly normal for an adult bedbug. They're also fairly immune to extremes of temperature. They're rumoured to be able to survive being run through the long cycle in a washing machine, which is why the recommended way of getting rid of them is by visual inspection as described above.

If you're concerned about being bitten, a closed sheet bag (AKA sleeping bag liner) offers some protection. Treating your sleeping bad and backpack with a chemical repellent (such as *Permethrin*) may also help. There are also now purpose-made anti-bedbug sleeping bag liners on the market, available in outdoor stores.

Bedbugs **are** a problem, and something that people get freaked out about, but it's important not to exaggerate the gravity of the situation. They're actually quite rare on the Camino and outbreaks are dealt with very promptly by the authorities. Many newer hostels are designed to be inhospitable to bedbugs (tiled floors, metal beds with mattresses in a plastic coating, bright colours, etc.) And generally there is no indication that the problem is getting worse.

In all my Caminos, I've only been bitten by bedbugs twice. Once was in the depth of winter in the Municipal hostel in Viana, where I was the only pilgrim. The little buggers must have been glad to see me because they had a field day. Although, it was nothing compared to my next encounter, which was thanks to one of those sweet old ladies who offer rooms to rent around Santiago. I shared a room with a friend of mine, who got straight into bed without showering and was snoring within minutes. In the morning, I found my upper body covered in bites. My friend had none. We high-tailed it out of there and found ourselves a cheap hotel. On both occasions I checked my belongings carefully and found nothing. The big red marks lasted quite a while. I think it took about a week before they were completely gone.

Are you scratching yourself yet?

TENDINITIS

Tendinitis means the inflammation of a tendon. Tendons are bands or strings of strong tissue, which connect muscles to bones. On the Camino, tendinitis usually occurs in the area of the ankle, where there are several important tendons for walking. It is usually caused by over-exertion. Symptoms include pain and stiffness. In extreme cases swelling may also be visible.

In mild cases, a course of oral anti-inflammatory drugs and rest may be sufficient to treat tendinitis. Cold compresses, bandages and elevating the affected area, may also help. Drinking loads of water can help to increase the natural lubrication in your tendons and joints. In more severe cases, medical attention is advised. Tendinitis can be caused and exacerbated by dehydration, so make sure you drink enough water.

MUSCLE PAIN

Muscle damage, causing pain and cramping, can happen as a result of overexertion. The best way of avoiding these problems is to pace yourself so your muscles and joints don't become overtired, and to pay attention to warning signs.

Stretching exercises, during and after your walking day, can also help to keep your muscles and joints healthy. Long-distance walkers commonly have problems of strain or cramping in their calf muscles. This is easy enough to avoid if you get in the habit of stretching those muscles regularly.

Stretching Stand about 1m from a wall, put your right foot forward about half way, bending your right knee. Put your hands against the wall and lean forward until you feel a gentle stretch in the calf muscles of your left leg. Held for a count of about 20. Now switch legs. Repeat as often as you find useful. (Type *stretch calf muscles* into *youtube.com* for examples.)

Stretching and strengthening Another useful exercise for your calves is; on a step or kerb, balance on your toes with your heels hanging over the edge. Now lift yourself up onto your toes, as high as you can go, then slowly lower yourself until your heels are as low as you can go and you can feel a stretch in your calves. Hold both positions for a few seconds. This exercise will strengthen and stretch those muscles. Repeat as often as you feel is appropriate.

KNEE PAIN

The Camino is hard on your knees, especially downhill sections. If you're experiencing any pain or discomfort in your knees, during or after your walking day, try the following. Lying flat on your back, lift one leg, bent at the knee, and grasp your leg with your hands around the ankle and pull it gently in to your body until your knee is fully bent. Hold for about 10 seconds before releasing. Repeat for both sides as often as you like.

I've had knee problems in the past. Not serious ones, but painful. I find a tubular knee bandage is excellent, and I always carry one. In fact I put in on for the long descents because it helps prevent pain starting in the first place. This, along with during- and post-walk stretching, keeps my knee problems under control.

INSECT BITES, ETC.

Mosquitoes in Spain aren't malaria carrying and so an annoyance rather than a danger. Pharmacies sell over-the-counter creams which will relieve discomfort and itching. Certain kinds of **ants** also bite, but are not dangerous. Watch where you sit. **Ticks** should be removed by a doctor to prevent infection. They are more common in moist climates such as Galicia. The recommended way to remove a tick is to use a fine-tipped tweezers, grip the tick as close to your skin as possible and pull outwards without jerking or twisting. Then check you got it all. The tried and trusted lighted cigarette method is frowned upon by the medical profession. Spain also has **bees** and **wasps**.

There are some poisonous snakes in Spain, living usually on the banks of rivers. If you get bitten, contact the emergency services – **112** – immediately.

HYPOTHERMIA

In winter, especially in mountainous area, there is a danger of hypothermia. This is defined as when the body's core temperature drops below 35°C (normal temperature is 36.5°C - 37.5°C). Severe cases, when core body temperature drops below 29°C, may cause heart palpitations and a sensation of being extremely hot, often causing victim to remove their clothing.

The treatment for hypothermia is to change the victim into dry clothing and warm them up as quickly as possible.

DIARRHOEA AND FOOD POISONING

Food poisoning is rare on the Camino, though mild diarrhoea is quite common and seems to mostly result from drinking spring or tap water, especially in the drier Meseta (G) section. If you're susceptible to stomach upsets, you might want to stick to bottled water or bring a supply of water purification tablets. In any case, switch to bottled water if you begin to experience digestive problems.

Diarrhoea can be treated with Imodium, which helps to regulate bowel movements. Care must be taken not to become dehydrated due to the extra fluid loss. It's also advisable to avoid oily food. Diarrhoea usually clears up within 2 to 3 days. If it lasts longer, or is accompanied by fever, it may be necessary to see a doctor.

The symptoms of **food poisoning** include vomiting, diarrhoea and possibly fever. Mild cases will clear up in 2 to 3 days. If symptoms persist beyond that, see a doctor.

FUNGAL INFECTIONS (ATHLETE'S FOOT)

Athlete's foot can be treated with a cream available from pharmacies (*nappy / diaper rash* cream basically) and (yeah) greater attention to personal hygiene.

HEAT-RASH

Heat-rash is an allergic reaction of the skin to excessive sweating. Its symptoms are multiple, evenly distributed, inflamed red lumps, usually on the upper body. It can easily be mistaken for bedbug bites. It can be treated with an over-the-counter oral antihistamine (Spanish *antihistamina*).

TOENAILS

Keep your toenails short to prevent them rubbing off your boots (especially on descents), which can cause painful injuries. This also cuts down on wear and tear on socks and boots.

FRICTION OR CHAFING RASH

This can occur between your legs or under your arms. A little hypo-allergenic moisturising cream will prevent it occurring and relieve symptoms.

The advice given in this book is designed to help you prevent injury and deal with minor injuries. It is not a substitute for professional medical advice. If you have any doubts about your ability to walk the Camino you should consult with your doctor. If, when on the Camino, pain or injury persists or is unbearable, you should seek professional medical help immediately.

Camino etiquette

The Camino has its own modes of behaviour, which you'll learn pretty quickly. The friendliness and openness of other pilgrims is one of the most wonderful things about the Camino. People talk to each other, help each other and generally behave towards each other with compassion and solidarity. There will, of course, be exceptions, but they remain rare. This strange, new environment can be intimidating so, here are a few suggestions to get you started.

Greet other pilgrims in Spanish, *Hola,* or *Buen Camino,* when passing by. Even if that's all the Spanish you know, people will appreciate your effort and respect for the local culture. Equally, when dealing with non-pilgrims make an effort with the language, even if it's just a few words. Spanish people are generally appreciative when people make an effort with their language (no matter how inept).

It is a widely-accepted tradition that, regardless which language you're speaking, the informal form of you is used among pilgrims of all ages. So, Spanish *tú* or *vosotros* instead of *Usted,* German *du* or *ihr* instead of *Sie* and (believe it or not) French *tu* instead of *vous.* A word of caution; although this tradition is widely accepted it is not *universally* accepted (or indeed known), so when in doubt, take your lead from native speakers.

In summer, pilgrims get up about 05:30 for a 06:00 start. In winter lie-ins until 08:00 aren't uncommon. If you really must start walking at a ridiculously early hour and in complete darkness, pack your stuff before you go to bed, so you can grab-and-go in the morning, thus minimising disturbance to people who want to sleep. There should be no reason to use your torch. This kind of inconsiderate behaviour has become such a problem during the summer that many hostels now forbid departures before 06:00.

Originally pilgrims only wore a cockle shell during their return journey from Santiago, to show that they had been there. Nowadays, most pilgrims do the return journey by some artificial means, and wear their cockle shell while they're walking to Santiago.

Another habit which persists from earlier times is that of leaving stones in piles along the side of the Camino. This probably served as a way of indicating the right direction in the days before the yellow arrows became so ubiquitous. While on some particularly lonely stretches of the Vía de la Plata it still serves this purpose, on the Camino Francés it has become more a symbol of solidarity.

Although people walk the Camino for many different reasons, ranging from the purely Roman Catholic, to the 'hoping to lose 10kg', generally there is a large degree of solidarity between pilgrims, helped by a common purpose, shared experiences and the 'hardship' of the road. So, while one person may be kneeling down to pray at the tomb of such-and-such a saint, another may be marvelling at the artwork, while yet another is wondering how many people went hungry to fund its construction. On the open road, and in the evening over a meal, an important part of the Camino is solidarity and respect. The Camino may sometimes be described as a 'Christian' or 'Catholic' pilgrimage, which it is of course, but it is also many other things besides.

Walking pilgrims and cyclists have a sometimes tense co-existence, not helped by the fact that some cyclists seem to be engaging in a macho, kamikaze race to make it to Santiago in as little time as possible. Cyclists would argue that walkers suffer from a sense of superiority, ignoring the fact that cyclists are continuing a long tradition of getting to Santiago by whatever means are available. So be accepting of our two-wheeled friends and keep your ears open for the warning rush of tyres on gravel, the *I'm coming through!* cling of a bicycle bell and the cry of *¡Bici! ¡Bici!* and be ready to get out of the way.

There is also sometimes tense co-existence between pilgrims walking unassisted and pilgrims with a back-up vehicle who some refer to as *turistas* (or sometimes also *turigrinos*, an amalgamation of the words for *tourist* and *pilgrim*). Rumours often circulate about individuals and groups having a car or a bus, and only walking some of the way or, not carrying their luggage. This leads to a certain amount of ill-feeling, especially during periods when accommodation may be scarce. You're bound to hear stories about arriving to find the hostel full of fresh-faced individuals with crisply ironed walking pants and improbably small backpacks. Although there is much pilgrim lore about this, the extent of the problem is exaggerated and the ill-feeling is misguided.

It is the tradition in Spain to walk sections of the Camino as part of an organised group, with a minibus to carry luggage. These groups may be parish pilgrimage associations, *Amigos del Camino* groups or *Cofradías / Confraternities*, all of whom do much voluntary work in aid of pilgrims, including running pilgrim hostels. So, when you see walking groups who you may feel are infringing on the tranquillity of *your Camino*, just remember these people are often the ones who raise money, run pilgrim hostels, sit on committees, pick up litter and do many other tasks which benefit us all, and ask for nothing in return.

Queuing (or *waiting in line*) etiquette varies greatly between different countries. In northern Europe and North America, a strict standing in a line and first come first serverd culture exists. That these customs are almost universally respected in those countries makes other people's customs seem chaotic, and (sometimes) not really like a queue at all. In Central and Eastern Europe, rather than standing in a line, people will tend to wait in a semi-circular formation. Although this can look like it isn't following any rules, in reality it is, and the first come first served rule is still respected. It's just that, when your turn comes, you have to be ready to take it, rather than it being automatic by virtue of being next in line.

You can imagine that bringing together a lot of people from lots of different countries in one place, where nobody's rules predominate, creates the potential for misunderstanding and conflict. That conflict happens very rarely is a tribute to the way pilgrims respect each other and respect the order of arrival. At times, in busier hostels, with *hospitaleros* who may be unused to working quickly, dealing with cash, etc., and where there may be a certain amount of competition (based on a perception of scarcity, which may be entirely imaginary), your patience will be tested, and you may feel other people are pushing in. However, this is nearly always as a result of misunderstanding by newer arrivals of who is already queuing. Gently pointing out to them that, *we're waiting too / nosotros estamos esperando tambien,* is usually enough to settle things. If you meet one of those rare creatures who just wants to be served first, you might consider just letting them. If they go on the Camino with that kind of attitude, then it's their loss.

Finally, on the final 100km you'll probably encounter some curiosity from new-comers about how long you've been walking, etc. Generally, Spanish people walking the last 100km have a great deal of respect for people who've walked much longer distances than they have. So, if you become the subject of curious questioning, remember the Spanish are a nation of talkative extroverts, who are generally very welcoming of pilgrims, and take it as for what it is, friendly curiosity and a degree of awe for people who would undertake such an arduous journey. And, whatever you do, don't tell them it was easy!

Smoking

2011 saw the introduction in Spain of a ban on smoking in public places, similar to the ban already in place in many other European countries. It covers cafés, restaurants and just about any enclosed public place. As in other countries, it is being widely respected. Other recent innovations to attempt to prise the population from their vices have included raising the minimum age at which you can buy tobacco products from 16 to 18, an increase in the cost of tobacco licences, meaning that places selling tobacco are sometimes scarce in rural areas and the introduction of an element of *supervision* to cigarette machines, which means in practice that a member of staff has to authorise each cigarette sale with the use of a remote control.

Drinking water

Tap water in Spain is generally safe to drink. Spanish water does not have the type of parasites which make unfiltered water unsafe in tropical countries. Public drinking fonts are common and are also safe, as long as there is not a sign stating otherwise (*Agus potable = drinking water, Agua no potable = not fit for human consumption*).

Bottled water is widely available and inexpensive.

See also Diarrhoea, etc. page 69.

Safety

The Camino is really very safe, and in modern times there have been very few reports of violent crime on it. It can be walked safely by anyone with a minimum of *street-*

smart. With a murder rate in modern times of zero, it's statistically safer than most urban areas.

The biggest dangers to life and limb are from getting run down crossing the road (you'll be reminded of this while you're there by the monuments to victims of traffic), and having a heart attack or stroke from pushing yourself too hard, usually in the hot afternoon sun (these victims sometimes get a monument too).

If you're walking along a road always, always walk on the left, facing oncoming traffic, so you can see what's coming and jump out of the way if they don't see you. Also, if you're walking at times of reduced visibility (especially during the winter), early in the morning or late at night, use a hi-viz jacket or torch (flashlight).

With the growth in the popularity of the Camino there has been a proliferation of massage and "alternative therapies" on offer. These are sometimes offered by a specific hostel. The provision of these services is entirely unregulated and, unfortunately, the quality varies to a huge degree. Prospective customers, especially women, need to exercise caution and trust their instincts, as there have been a few reports of massage sessions turning out to be "groping sessions". It's a good idea to make sure a friend is present at any massages / therapies, to deter and assist.

Women

As a man it's difficult to know what to say to a woman who's worried about her personal safety on the Camino.

It's easy to quote statistics and say that the number of murders on the Camino in recent times is zero. That the number of (reported) sexual assaults is tiny. That, considering the number of people who walk the Camino every year, the level of violence in general is extremely low. That, it's entirely possibly you're safer on the Camino than in your home town.

But statistics, while good for giving us a rational basis for overcoming fear, aren't always that effective at helping people feel less afraid.

Perhaps the best argument against letting fear stop you doing this is precedent. The precedent that thousands of women every year walk the Camino and come to no harm. The fact that, if you look around the internet you'll find many, many accounts of women, young, old, on their own, in groups, walking the Camino and overwhelmingly reporting positive experiences. If you ask you'll easily find women, experienced pilgrims, who'll be happy to tell you, don't be afraid, just go.

Theft

Petty theft isn't common on the Camino, but it's a good idea to have **good security habits** when it comes to more **valuable items** such as cameras, phones, music players, credit cards, cash, passports, etc. Your other belonging such as clothes, boots, etc. will be pretty safe. Hostels don't provide lockers, so pilgrims generally leave their backpack and other belongings on or beside their bed.

The safest strategy with your valuables is to keep them with you at all times. This is where a **waterproof money-belt** or some other kind of **pouch** or **small bag** comes in handy. One that you can keep with you at all times (including when you take a shower), and take into your sleeping bag at night, or tuck under your pillow.

Regardless of how you organise yourself, it's important to get in the habit of not leaving your valuables lying around and, if you have to leave them somewhere, putting them out of sight.

Remember: Most petty theft is unplanned and opportunistic.

Or even better, leave non-essential items such as expensive smartphones, cameras, iWhatevers, etc., at home. This goes back to the **Golden Rule of Packing:** will I really NEED this to walk the Camino?

Another problem with expensive electronic equipment is that in most hostels you'll have to leave it in a public place to charge. This leaves you with a dilemma, take the risk of leaving it unattended, or waste time (possibly) every day watching over it.

PLAN B

It's also important to have a **Plan B,** in case the worst happens. Think through what you would need to do if your passport, cash cards or credit cards were stolen. Do you know the phone number of someone who could help you? Or have you got contact details recorded someplace where you can retrieve them easily? Is there somebody who could wire you money? How? (See **Western Union** under Banking and Money, page 57.) Have you got a photocopy of the photo page of your passport? Do you know what number to call to cancel your cards? Do you know your credit card and bank account numbers? Is there some reliable person you can leave emergency information with?

Are your smartphone's screen lock and start-up passwords enabled? Is it set up so you can wipe it remotely? These options are available on most modern smartphones.

If you take basic precautions you're unlikely to be a victim of crime, and you'll have the peace of mind of knowing that if the worst does happen, you have a plan in place for dealing with it. A state of permanent paranoia would take from your experience and enjoyment of the Camino. So take the precautions, and don't worry.

In all the Caminos I've walked, I have never had anything stolen, and I'm not even that careful with my stuff. I confess, I don't follow to the letter the advice I just gave you above (although, it is good advice). I don't take everything into the shower with me, I have a waterproof wallet for documents and cards which is in the pocket of my shorts (suitable pockets is the deciding factor for me when choosing Camino pants!) and which stays with me at all times. Other stuff, like camera and phone, I usually stash in the bottom of my backpack. My logic is, that nobody is going to go searching around in the bottom of a backpack in a busy dorm, with pilgrims coming and going all the time, on the off chance that someone left something valuable there (nobody would be that stupid).

That's not to say I haven't been robbed in Spain. I have! In Barcelona main railway station. I put my sleeping bag down beside me on a bench and when I went to put it back in my backpack it was gone. So, maybe the time to be more careful of your belongings is on the way to and on the way home from the Camino.

Dogs

Along the Camino Francés, dogs generally aren't a problem; they see so many bedraggled characters wandering past their door every day that they don't even bother barking any more.

If you do meet an aggressive dog, your safest option is to back away (without turning your back) and get out of its territory. Running is not a good idea because many breeds of dogs will instinctively take chase. It's also probable the dog's owner is someplace nearby, and attracting their attention would be the easiest way to deal with the offending mutt.

If none of these options are practical, then raising a stick at it will probably be enough to convince it it's dealing with someone who'll fight back (working, country dogs associate a stick with pain, unlike their townie cousins). If you haven't got a stick to hand, bend down and pick up a few stones; they understand that too.

However, hitting the dog is an absolute last resort, only to be used if it attacks first. Pre-emptive action may just provoke it.

If you encounter dogs looking after sheep or goats, bear in mind that they're quite protective and if you come between them and their flock they will regard you as a threat. So don't approach them and avoid walking between them and their charges.

If you're worried about dogs another possibility is to carry some kind of dog-repelling spray. These are available online and from pet shops. There are different varieties from the fairly mild to the potentially lethal. If you're buying a spray bear in mind they are not legal in every country and may even be regarded as a weapon by customs.

Having said that, dogs aren't a problem on the Camino I'd love to say I've never been attacked by one. Unfortunately, I can't. But in all the Caminos I've walked it only happened once, and that was on a remote and little-frequented stretch of the Chemin d'Arles, *in the French Pyrenees. I was walking along a quiet road with a farm house on my right. There were three large dogs in the farmyard and the gate was open, so I was immediately on my guard. I had passed the gate by the time they saw me. They immediately started barking and two of them ran out. I turned with my stick in my hand to face them. They were huge slobbering mongrels, about the size of small horses, but they backed off when I faced them down. I took a step towards them and they retreated to the gate. Thinking myself safe, I made the mistake of turning my back on them. I'd only gone a couple of steps when I felt something grab the back of my leg. I turned at once and swung my stick, but the so-and-so had already scampered. I retreated, pausing at a safe distance to inspect the damage. My pants were ripped, but luckily he hadn't managed to bite me with any force. The skin was broken but the wound was basically a scratch. I took a photo of the offending beast and headed on my way.*

In the next village the chain-smoking local doctor scoffed at my injury, in typical French fashion, and assured me I would live and that my worries about la rage / rabies *were without foundation. He did however insist I report the incident to the police. Which I did, despite my reluctance, given my slightly scruffy appearance. The Gendarmes, to their credit, were friendly and helpful and took the matter seriously, noted the culprit's description from the photo I'd taken of him and, peering into my camera's tiny screen, promised to "deal with him" ("On va s'occuper de lui"), in a tone of voice which made me feel pangs of regret for the animal which, in all likelihood, had only wanted to give me a nip and could have take my leg off if he'd tried. When I protested that it wasn't that serious, they chuckled among themselves and assured me that they were just going to speak to the owner and make sure he kept his dogs under control in future.*

Relieved, I hurried on my way before they took another look at me and decided to lock me up for vagrancy. That evening, a nice Swiss pilgrim produced a sewing kit from the bottom of her backpack and fixed my pants like new. I got another couple of years out of those pants and, whenever anybody asked me about the torn leg, I told them about my brush with death in the French Pyrenees.

Police and emergency services (112)

As in other EU countries, dialling **112** connects you to an emergency operator who can then connect you to the police, ambulance service, fire brigade, etc. You can dial 112 from any phone for free. If you dial it from your mobile when it's not connect to a network, it will attempt to connect you through any available network. The emergency operator will be able to speak English or will quickly pass you to someone who does.

Spain has several different police forces: the **Guardia Civil** is a national force with a strong military style ethos. They're in charge of national security, border security, traffic enforcement and general policing, outside of urban areas with more than 10,000 inhabitants (so, most of the Camino). Their fortified barracks always have the motto, *Todo por la Patria / Everything for the Motherland,* above the entrance.

In urban areas with more than 10,000 inhabitants the **Policía Local** are in charge. This is a more conventional police force, focused on community policing. The Policía Local is called different things in different regions. In Navarra it's the **Policía Foral**, and in the Basque Country it's the **Ertzaintza**. Some smaller towns have a **Policía Municipal,** who take care of community policing. All police in Spain carry guns.

Posting unwanted 'weight' to Santiago

If you want to have some extra clothes for when you arrive in Santiago, or you find after you've started the Camino (having ignored all the advice in this book!) that you're carrying too much weight, you can always send it to Santiago from any post office and pick it up when you arrive there.

From inside Spain it will cost about (2013 prices):

5kg = 5,99€, 10kg = 8,83€, 15kg = 10,89€

It can be forwarded to *poste restante* (general delivery) / *Lista de Correos* in the post office in Santiago. If you're sending it from a point on the Camino the people in the post office will be able to advise you. Post offices also sell boxes.

If you don't want to send it to *poste restante*, there's a service in Santiago which will store it for you, for a small price. Their website also has quite a bit of useful information about shipping luggage to Santiago.

See *caminodesantiago.me/luggage-storage-in-santiago-de-compostela*

Baggage transport services

Many people chose to have their backpack transported for them, along the whole way or just part of it. You'll see many ads along the Camino and in hostels for various services. Generally they work together with private hostels and will drop your bag at the hostel of your choice and sometimes also make a reservation for you.

From Saint-Jean **Express Bourricot** provide a baggage service. See their website: *www.expressbourricot.com.*

In Spain there are several companies which provide this service:

Camino Fácil *www.caminofacil.net*   Jacotrans *www.jacotrans.com*

THE CAMINOS

Since pilgrimage to Santiago first began over a millennium ago, the routes pilgrims follow have taken on a special significance. With the explosion in popularity of the Camino in recent decades, there is renewed interest in the history of these routes. Now many of them, not just in the Iberian Peninsula, but as far away as Central and Eastern Europe, are being documented and waymarked, and recognised as Caminos in their own right.

Spain and Portugal

All of the Caminos listed below are waymarked and have an infrastructure of pilgrim hostels.

CAMINO FRANCÉS

The *Camino Francés*, or *French Way*, is the traditional name for the Camino which runs from the French border to Santiago. Today, as through much of the Middle Ages, this is the busiest and best-know Camino de Santiago.

A free guide to the Camino Francés is available from *www.caminoguide.net*.

VÍA DE LA PLATA

The *Vía de la Plata* was originally a Roman Road which linked the Mediterranean port of Cadiz with the silver mines of Asturias hence its name, the *Silver Route*.

The present day Vía follows the route of this Roman Road for part of its length. It is traditionally considered to start in either Seville or Mérida, and it follows the route of the Roman Road as far as Granja de Moreruela, in the province of Zamora, where it splits, the left route goes through the mountains of southern Galicia (see **Camino Sanabrés** below) to reach Santiago from the south, while the right route continues northwards, joining the Camino Francés in Astorga.

A free guide is available from *www.viadelaplataguide.net*. If you're interested in the *Vía de la Plata* the **Amigos del Camino de Santiago de Sevilla** run a useful website at *www.viaplata.org*. **Godesalco** also has loads of information *www.godesalco.com*.

CAMINO SANABRÉS

The Camino Sanabrés starts in Granja de Moreruela, where it branches from the Vía de la Plata, passes through southern Galicia and ends in Santiago. When modern pilgrims refer to the Vía de la Plata they're usually referring to a combination of it and the Camino Sanabrés.

A free guide is available from *www.viadelaplataguide.net*.

CAMINO ARAGONÉS

The Camino Aragonés is the name sometimes used for the Spanish section of the *Chemin d'Arles* (see below). It starts at the Spanish border, at the Col de Somport, passes through Jaca and joins the Camino Francés in Eunate, near Puente la Reina.

A free guide is available from *www.caminoguide.net.*

CAMINO DEL BAZTÁN

The Camino del Baztán, starts in Bayonne in South West France and goes due south, through the beautiful Baztán Valley of northern Navarra, to join the Camino Francés just before Pamplona. In recent years its infrastructure of pilgrim accommodation has improved greatly, and it is now possible to walk this little-known Camino, staying in pilgrim hostels, with no difficulties.

A free guide is available from *www.caminoguide.net.*

CAMINO DEL INVIERNO

The Winter Way splits from the Camino Francés in Ponferrada and follows a more southerly, less mountainous route, through Galicia, before joining the Camino Sanabrés in Lalín, for the last couple of days into Santiago. There is no guide in English as yet, but a leaflet in Spanish and map, may be available from the tourist office in Ponferrada. It is said to be walkable with relative ease, using a mixture of pilgrim and tourist accommodation.

CAMINO INGLÉS

The *Camino Inglés* or *English Way*, is the route traditionally followed by pilgrims who arrived by ship to Ferrol or A Coruña. It arrives in Santiago from the north.

CAMINO DEL NORTE / CAMINO DE LA COSTA

The Camino del Norte starts at the French border, at Irún, in the Basque Country. It follows the north coast closely, before turning south east in Galicia to join the Camino Francés near Arzúa. This was the most commonly used route during the early days of the Camino.

CAMINO PRIMITIVO / RUTA JACOBEA PRIMITIVA

The Camino Primitivo splits from the Camino del Norte about 30km before Oviedo, and follows an inland, mountainous route, passing through Lugo to join the Camino Francés in Palas de Rei. This is considered to be the original Camino because it is the route used by King Alfonso II to travel to Santiago, having heard that St James' remains had been discovered there. It's quite mountainous but very beautiful.

CAMINO PORTUGUÉS

The Camino Portugués begins in the very south of Portugal, but most modern pilgrims start in Oporto. It crosses from Portugal into Galicia to arrive in Santiago from the south.

VÍA LUSITANA

The Vía Lusitana starts on the south coast of Portugal, at the mouth of the Guardiana River, and follows an inland route north, to join the Camino Sanabrés in Galicia. It is sparsely waymarked and there is little pilgrim accommodation. The only guidebook (*Via Lusitana von der Algarve nach Ourense*) is in German, published by Outdoor and available on Amazon.

CAMINO MOZÁRABE

The Camino Mozárabe (G) starts in Granada and passes through Córdoba, to join the Vía de la Plata in Mérida.

CAMINO DEL EBRO

The Camino del Ebro follows the River Ebro from its estuary in Catalonia and joins the Camino Francés in Logroño.

Throughout Europe

The Caminos don't start at the Spanish border. All over Europe there are traditional paths pointing towards the south west, all with a strong heritage of pilgrimage. In recent years many of these have been 'rediscovered' and are now being developed with guidebooks, waymarkings and hostels.

CHEMIN DE TOURS

The Chemin de Tours (Latin: *Via Turonensis*) is the main route from northern France, Benelux, northern Germany and points north. Today the traditional starting point is Tours. It connects up with the Camino Francés or the Camino del Norte.

CHEMIN DE VÉZELAY

The Chemin de Vézelay or Voie de Vézelay (Latin: *Via Lemosina)* was the main route from North-Eastern France and central Germany. It joins the Camino Francés in Ostabat.

CHEMIN DU PUY

The Chemin du Puy (Latin: *Via Podiensis*) is the main route from southern Germany, Switzerland, Austria, and points east although today the traditional starting point is Le Puy-en-Velay. It is traditionally considered the most difficult route because it passes through the mountainous Massif Central. Today it is the most popular of the French Caminos.

CHEMIN D'ARLES

The Chemin d'Arles (Latin: *Via Tolosana*) is the main route from southern France, Italy and south east Europe. It connects to the Camino Aragonés at the Col de Somport.

Literature of the Camino

The Road to Santiago by *Walter Starkie,* is an informative and entertaining account of Mr Starkie's various journeys along the roads to Santiago between the 1930s and 1950s, drawing on his extensive knowledge of the history and architecture of the Caminos, and of the peoples who live along them.

The Pilgrimage Road to Santiago by *David M. Gitlitz,* is a encyclopaedic description of the history and architecture of the Camino, its major churches and cathedrals, works of art and religious iconography.

The Pilgrimage: A Contemporary Quest for Ancient Wisdom by *Paulo Coelho.* Either you love him or you just find him completely incomprehensible, either way he needs no introduction. In Spanish it's called **El Peregrino: Diario de un mago.**

Buen Camino! A Father-Daughter Journey from Croagh Patrick to Santiago De Compostela: by *Natasha* and *Peter Murtagh.* Starting on Ireland's holy mountain, Croagh Patrick, with each writing alternate chapters, father and daughter tell the story of their Camino and an entertaining and readable format. Based on the Camino in 2012, so very contemporary.

El Peregrino (in Spanish) by *Jesús Torbado*, is a fictionalised account of a medieval French pilgrim's journey to Santiago in an attempt to save his home village from the Plague (G). Along the way, he encounters thieves, charlatans, sadistic monks and sex-starved nuns. Eventually he meets his true love, and settles down with her near Villafranca del Bierzo, only to have their happiness end in tragedy. Written in conversational Spanish, so great for learners.

Pilgerstab und Jakobmuschel (in German) by *Norbert Ohler*, is an exhaustively researched history of pilgrimage in Europe. It deals with the social, economic, cultural and religious aspects of all major pilgrimage routes, from their beginnings to the present day. The author has written extensively on religious life and travel in the Middle Ages. Some of his books are available in English but unfortunately not this one.

Ich bin dann mal weg (in German) by *Hape Kerkling*, available in English under the (only slightly long-winded) title **I'm Off Then: Losing and Finding Myself on the Camino de Santiago**. A popular German comedian's account of his adventures on the Camino Francés. This book stayed at the top of the German best seller list for 50 weeks. Mr Kerkling only stayed in hotels, seemed to have disliked most of his fellow pilgrims, and the only thing he really got excited about was stray dogs.

Les Chemins de St Jacques (in French) by *Yves Bottineau*, is an entertaining and comprehensive history of pilgrimage to Santiago, covering all angles but with a special emphasis on architecture.

Nature

The Camino Francés passes through a diverse landscape, from the mountainous Pyrenees to the flatness of the Meseta (G) after Sahagún and finally the rolling hills of Galicia. It also passes through several distinct climate zones as the region straddles the fringes of the Atlantic and Mediterranean climates. These changes can be discerned in the vegetation you see around you.

The Pyrenees (Spanish: *Pirineos*, Basque: *Pirinioak*, French: *Pyrenées*) is the mountain range which geographically isolates the Iberian Peninsula from the rest of Europe. The Pyrenees were formed by the expansion of the Bay of Biscay pushing the Iberian landmass in a pivoting motion into France. Because of their relative youth (although they're older than the Alps), and the abundance of hard limestone, the Pyrenees are relatively uneroded. The western part of the Pyrenees between Saint-Jean and Roncesvalles, is low compared to the high Pyrenees, further to the east, where the highest point is the 3,404m **Aneto** in eastern Aragon. As it traverses the Pyrenees the Camino reaches a maximum altitude of 1,430m. This region is noted for a moderate **Atlantic climate** with **heavy rainfall** and **strong winds**. **Snowfall** is also possible, and sometimes abundant, on high ground in winter. Flora is of Atlantic type with heavy **pine forests** up to about 800m. Although walking through the mountains only takes a day, the foothills continue as far as Zubiri.

Navarra and La Rioja are characterised by rolling hills and the cultivation of wheat and vines (grapes) and wine production. Atlantic flora continues about as far as the **Alto del Perdón** where it is abruptly replaced by **Mediterranean**.

The Meseta is the name given to the high plains of Spain's interior. It is divided by the Sistema Central mountain range into northern and southern halves. The altitude of the Meseta fluctuates between 600m and 800m. It has a **dry Mediterranean climate, hot** in summer and **cold** in winter when snow is not uncommon. The Camino crosses the northern-most fringe of the Northern Meseta, never straying more than about 100km from the mountain range which stand between the Meseta and the north coast. The Northern Meseta stretches south as far as the Sistema Central mountains, which are visible from Madrid. It is drained by the Duero river system, which enters the Atlantic at Porto in Portugal. It is intensively farmed, the principal crop being wheat.

North West León starts after **Astorga** and brings you once again into mountainous territory and an **Atlantic climate.** Here wind, rain and snow are experienced in abundance during the winter and the flora becomes Atlantic type again, with some **pine forests.** The broad valley of **El Bierzo,** with its **mild micro-climate,** has intensive cultivation of fruit and vegetables. It is also a major vine growing and wine producing region. Subsistence agriculture is still common in upland areas.

Galicia has a classic **mild Atlantic climate** with **strong winds** and **interminable rain** possible in all seasons. Winters are mild and summers are cool. Vegetation is abundant and lush. Galicia has the highest percentage of **forest cover** of any region in Spain. **Eucalyptus** trees, brought here from Australia in the 19th century, now cover large areas. Eucalyptus and pine trees are highly valued for their fast growth rate. However, over-cultivation of Eucalyptus has had a detrimental effect on local biodiversity and water supply. Because of its abundance in trees, Galicia is one of the regions of Spain most at danger from **forest fires.**

Architecture

It's important to remember when trying to identify the architectural category to which a particular building belongs, that most buildings were constructed over a period of decades, and sometimes centuries, and usually with several different architects and patrons at different times, and may have been partially or entirely rebuilt or added to. Consequently, it is not always appropriate to speak of a single architectural style or influence.

The craftsmen who built medieval buildings often carved identifying marks on stones or wood. Stones were also marked to indicate where they belonged on the building, their dimension, the direction they should face, etc.

NB. figures in brackets are centuries.

Iberian (Before 3rd BC) surviving traces of pre-Roman buildings in Spain are of similar design to elsewhere in Europe. They are believed to have been mostly of a ceremonial nature such as the burial mounds in Antequera. They were built of large stones which were hauled into place and then buried.

Celtic (2nd BC – 3rd AD) settlers in Spain typically built fortified villages called Castros. The remains of a number of these can still be seen in the valley of the Duero and Galicia. These were stone houses, usually circular or oblong, with a thatched roof.

Roman (3rd BC – 6th AD) The Romans introduced new building methods and styles when they arrived in the third century BC. These included the arch and the dome, which made possible the construction, on a scale previously impossible, of bridges and aqueducts and large covered public spaces, such as the **bath houses** and

amphitheatres with which they adorned their cities. The best surviving amphitheatres in Spain is in **Mérida**, on the **Vía de la Plata**. However, possibly their greatest achievement was a road network which connected all corners of their empire. Several parts of the Camino Francés follow Roman roads (Spanish *Calzada Romana*).

Moorish (8th – 15th) the Muslim invaders brought with them a rich architectural heritage from North Africa and Arabia. In **al-Andalus,** they developed a new style which adopted influences from the **Romans** and the **Visigoths**. Their buildings are plain on the outside, symmetrical in shape with interiors decorated with ornate and intricate tiling with much calligraphy and depictions of animals and birds (people being absent due to Islam's interdiction of the portrayal of the human form). Their palaces are usually surrounded by stately gardens, with sophisticated systems of flowing water and fountains. Most examples of this type of architecture are in Southern Spain, where Muslim influence was strongest.

Mozarabic (G) (10th – 13th) is a term used to describe a style of building invented by Mozarabic migrants from southern to northern Spain during the Reconquista (G). Examples of it are mostly found in the valley of the Duero and other regions where they settled. It is characterised by a general external simplicity and **horseshoe arches** above doors and windows (arches which are slightly more than a half circle). Arches were also often enclosed by a rectangular frame *(alfiz)*.

Romanesque (10th – 13th) architecture came to Spain from France and its commonness along the **Camino Francés** suggests that this was its main entry point. Churches built in this style typically have very thick walls, few windows, round arches and round vaulted ceilings. The ceiling over the aisles and nave are generally of similar height.

Gothic (12th – 16th) architecture came from France in the 12th century. It introduced the pointed arch and external supports, allowing buildings to be taller, with bigger windows. Carved decoration is also typical of this architectural style. **León** and **Burgos cathedrals** are good examples of this style and Burgos is known for its Gothic architecture.

Mudéjar (G) (12th – 16th) architecture is a fusion of **Moorish** with **Romanesque, Gothic** and **Renaissance** styles. It is characterised by the extensive use of brick and elaborate decorations using tiles, brickwork, wood carving, plaster carving and ornamental metals. Many of the finest examples of Mudéjar building are found in Aragon and Andalusia.

Renaissance (15th – 16th) architecture came to Spain from **Italy**. It revived classical Roman styles with updated influences. It has a refined sense of symmetry and makes use of the round arches and columns.

Herrerian architectural constitutes a subclass of **Renaissance** architecture. It is characterised by clean, straight lines and a lack of decoration. In contrast with Baroque, buildings built in this style are recognisable for their bareness.

Plateresque (15th – 16th) architecture is a subset of **Renaissance** architecture. Its name comes from plata meaning silver because its characteristic ornately detailed decoration resembles silver. (See: Hostal de San Marcos under León).

Baroque (17th – 18th) architecture is a very ornamental, curving style with its origins in the **Counter-Reformation** (G), when the Catholic Church used graphic and emotive images from the Bible in art and architecture, to engage with and educate its followers. The western façade of **Santiago Cathedral,** which overlooks Praza do Obradoiro, is a good example of this style.

Rococo (18th) is a style of art and design originating in France. Its principal features are elegant and ornate decoration, small sculptures, mirrors, reliefs and wall paintings.

Modern (20th onwards) Modern Spanish architecture has its roots in Barcelona in the late 19th century. One of its most famous designers was Gaudí (G), whose magnificent Episcopal Palace can be visited in Astorga. In its earlier phases, it is distinguished by its use of undulating shapes and spirals. More recent designers, such as Calatrava, whose single-span bridges with cable supports have won him fame, make imaginative use of modern materials and building methods to produce distinctive and original structures.

Each of the **euro banknotes** has an example of a different architectural style:
5€ = Classical, 10€ = Romanesque, 20€ = Gothic, 50€ = Renaissance, 100€ = Baroque and Rococo, 200€ = Iron and glass, 500€ = Modern.

For other architectural terms see:
en.wikipedia.org/wiki/Glossary_of_architecture

REGIONAL ARCHITECTURE ON THE CAMINO

Along the Camino there are many fine examples of architecture both ancient and modern in various historical and regional styles. Traditional regional building methods persisted in some places into the 20th century due to lack of economic development and geographic isolation. In these styles, all of the material used is locally sourced.

Starting in **Saint-Jean** until about **Estella, Basque architecture** dominates and, in the villages through which you will pass, there are many examples of the traditional Basque farmhouses.

The houses of **La Rioja** are brick and stone built, reflecting locally available building material and prosperity based on the wine trade.

In the **Meseta,** where stones are scarce, houses were built from adobe bricks plastered with a smooth coating of mud. The bricks are made by mixing clay with straw and then allowing them to dry in the sun. The construction of the walls can be seen clearly in the numerous derelict buildings which bear witness to the region's dwindling population.

In the mountainous regions after **Astorga,** houses have thick stone walls to conserve heat during the cold winters, and in **Galicia** houses often have overhanging roofs and balconies to afford some protection from the interminable rains of winter.

Statistics of the Camino

The statistics shown relate to **2015,** unless otherwise stated. Figures for earlier years are given by way of comparison. Remember, **2010** was a *Holy Year / Año Santo.*

PILGRIMS ARRIVING IN SANTIAGO
Total pilgrims arriving in Santiago each year, all Caminos

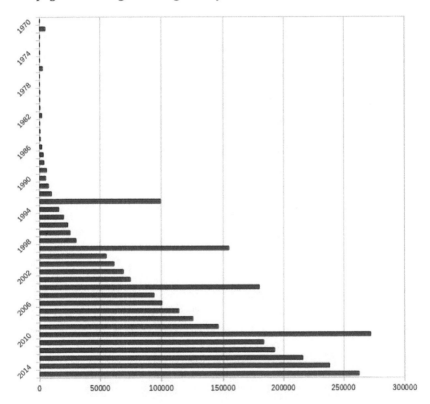

The Camino reached a statistical nadir in 1978 when the ecclesiastical authorities in Santiago recorded a total of 13 pilgrims. This number has increased massively since then, reaching a peak of 272,135 in Holy Year 2010, before falling back to 183,366 in 2011 and then increasing by 43% over the next five years to 262,515 in 2015. While the figure for 2010 is impressive of itself (and a record in the recent history of the Camino), it was the first **Holy Year** when the total number of pilgrims was less than double the total for the preceding year (it was 186%), indicating that the difference between normal years and Holy Years is decreasing.

PILGRIMS DEPARTING SAINT-JEAN-PIED-DE-PORT

Pilgrims departing Saint-Jean-Pied-de-Port by year

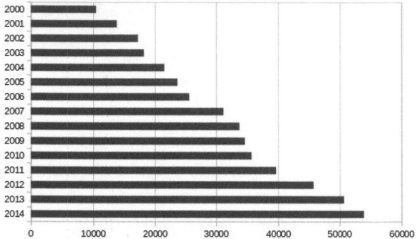

The organisation which helps pilgrims in Saint-Jean-Pied-de-Port, *les Amis du Chemin de Saint-Jacques de Compostelle*, also keeps a count of departing pilgrims. The above graph is based on this. In 2014, they recorded a total of 53,972 pilgrims departing Saint-Jean (an increase of 6.4% on 2013, down from an increase of 11% for 2013/2012). Compare this to 31,057 arriving in Santiago having started in Saint-Jean and we can see that about 40% of pilgrims who start in Saint-Jean don't walk to Santiago. This is mostly because they never intended to, rather than some misfortune befalling them.

What's most striking about this graph is that it shows that the number of pilgrims starting in Saint-Jean is almost completely unaffected by Holy Years (ie. 2010).

POPULAR STARTING POINTS FOR ARRIVALS IN SANTIAGO

Percentages given are: (% of total Camino Francés)

Sarria	67,421	(39.1%)
Saint-Jean-Pied-de-Port	31,057	(18%)
León	11,496	(6.7%)
O Cebreiro	10,354	(6%)
Ponferrada	8,402	(4.9%)
Roncesvalles	7,419	(4.3%)
Astorga	6,034	(3.5%)
Pamplona	4,640	(2.7%)

STARTING POINTS TRENDS

As the graph below illustrates, the number of people starting in Sarria is increasing, reflecting the growing popularity of walking the last 100km. Saint-Jean-Pied-de-Port is also increasing while the number for Roncesvalles is decreasing.

Notable in the graph below is the effect of Holy Year 2010 on the numbers departing Sarria and its much weaker effect on Roncesvalles and Saint-Jean-Pied-de-Port.

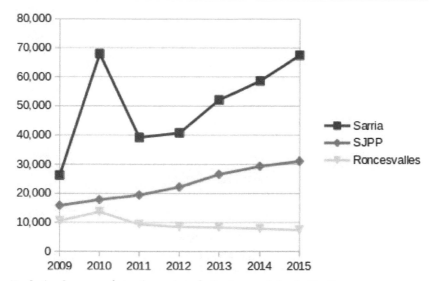

Evolution by year of starting point of pilgrims arriving in Santiago

PILGRIMS' COUNTRIES OF ORIGIN

For 2015, percentages given are (% of total 2014 / % of total 2015)

Spain	122,377	(47.8% / 46.6%)	Italy	22,124	(8.5% / 8.4%)
Germany	18,859	(6.9% / 7.2%)	USA	13,659	(4.9% / 5.2%)
Portugal	12,465	(4.9% / 4.8%)	France	9,914	(3.9% / 3.8%)
UK	5,415	(1.9% / 2.1%)	Ireland	5,360	(2.1% / 2%)
Korea	4,072	(1.6% / 1.5%)	Australia	3,855	(1.6% / 1.5%)
Canada	4,201	(1.5% / 1.6%)			

In a sign of the continuing internationalisation of the Camino, the percentage of Spanish pilgrims in the total arriving in Santiago fell below 50% in 2012 and is still falling. Unsurprisingly, they're still by far the biggest nationality, well ahead of the Italians in second place with 8.4%.

The numbers of pilgrims from all of the leading countries increased between 2014 and 2015. However, in percentage terms Italy, Portugal, Ireland and Australia all decreased. This reflects the increasing diversity in pilgrims' nationalities with just about all of the eastern Europe countries, as well as Russia (873) and China (706), increasing strongly.

CULTURAL PREVALENCE

To illustrate the cultural prevalence of the Camino in different countries we calculate the number of people of each nationality who walked the Camino (based on arrivals in Santiago) in 2015 per 100,000 of populated. eg.

Spanish pilgrims = 122,366, Spain's population = 40,000,000*

So 122,366 / 40,000,000 * 100,000 = 306 (2014 was 284)

2014's figure is given in brackets.

So for every 100,000 Spanish nationals 306 (284) walked the Camino to Santiago in 2015. This is by far the highest prevalence of any country. The next highest is Portugal with 113 (106) followed by Ireland* with 89 (84), then Italy with 37 (34) and Germany with 24 (20) and France with 15 (14). Of the English speaking countries Canada's is 12 (10), Australia's is 17 (16), the UK's is 9 (7) and the USA's is 4 (4).

Spain's population is estimated at 40,000,000, excluding foreign residents. Ireland's population is estimated at 6,000,000. 4,000,000 excluding foreign residents, in the Irish Republic and 2,000,000 outside it.

WHICH ROUTE PEOPLE WALKED

For 2014 (% change 2013 / 2014)

Camino Francés 172,244 (6.8% / 6.3%) Camino Portugués 43,149 (20.1% / 21.5%) Camino del Norte 15,873 (12.7% / 5.2%) Camino Primitivo 11,428 (20.7% / 38.1%) Camino Inglés 9,247 (63.5% / 28.4%) Vía de la Plata 9,221 (-5.8% / 8.6%) Other Caminos 1,339 (52% / -2.2%)

The trend towards alternatives to the Camino Francés continues. The biggest growers were the Camino Inglés, Camino Primitivo and the Camino Portugués. The Vía de la Plata grew again after declining from 2013 to 2014.

PILGRIM ARRIVALS BY MONTH

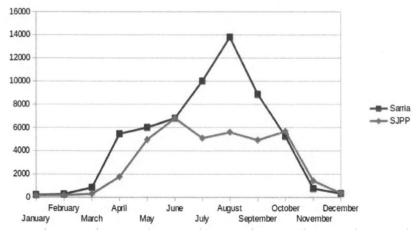

Arrivals in Santiago who started in Sarria and Saint-Jean-Pied-de-Port (2013)
The number of people walking from Sarria gives an indication of the busy months on the last 100km. The number of people walking from Saint-Jean gives an indication of activity on the rest of the Camino.

The first jump in numbers from Sarria coincides with Easter (March). The Sarria numbers climb steeply in July and August and decline steeply in September, October and November. While the Saint-Jean numbers remain more-or-less consistent throughout the summer, until October when they decline sharply. One interesting change in the Saint-Jean numbers is that October is now the second busiest month, whereas in the past this was usually August. This reflects the fact that more people are starting from Saint-Jean in September.

DIFFERENCE BETWEEN HOLY YEARS AND OTHER YEARS

Walking in a Holy Year has a different feel to walking in any other year. The pilgrims walking have quite a different profile, with far more walking in groups and walking for purely religious reasons. These are reflected in a statistical comparison between **2009** and **Holy Year 2010**.

While the age profile varied little between the two years, the percentage travelling by **bicycle** was lower in 2010 (12.22%) than in 2009 (17.06%). There was also a slightly higher percentage of **women** in 2010 (44.33%) than in 2009 (41.09%).

Unsurprisingly, the motivational profile of pilgrims shows a much higher percentage walking for **Religious** reasons (2009: 42.6%, 2010: 54.5%), and a lower percentage (although a higher headcount) in both other categories, with the numbers citing a **Not religious** motivation remaining almost identical.

The profile by **nationality** also differs sharply, with Spaniards making up 54.16% of pilgrims in 2009, against 69.16% in 2010. The fact that the Spanish are more inclined to walk just the last 100km is reflected in the statistics for starting points. The interesting thing to note about starting points is that while in 2010 almost a quarter of pilgrims started in Sarria (and just walked the last 100km), the headcount for starting points earlier on the Camino aren't hugely different from 2009. This means that numbers along most of the Camino are largely unaffected by a Holy Year, while the bit at the end is even more crowded than usual.

MOTIVATION

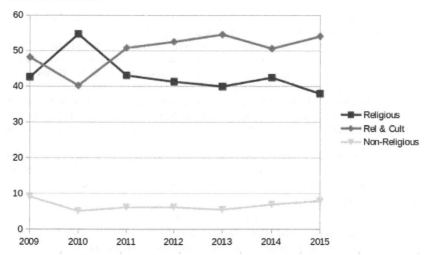

Recorded motivation of pilgrims arriving into Santiago
Besides Holy Year 2010 the figures are remarkably unchanging.

PILGRIMS' AGES AND GENDER

Under 30: 28.5%; 30 to 60: 54.8%; Over 60: 16.7%
A small increase in over 60s and under 30s compared to 2014.
Men: 53%; Women: 47%. The percentage of female walkers increased by 1%.

HISTORY

History of Spain

PREHISTORIC IBERIA

The earliest traces of habitation by the ancestors of humans in Spain were uncovered during the construction of a railway, very close to the Camino Francés, in Burgos Province. Excavations at this site have uncovered human remains and artefacts dating back to the early **Stone Age**, in sufficient abundance to make this one of the most important archaeological sites in the world. The finds include rock paintings, tools, remains of lions and bison, and possible evidence, in the form of chewed human bones, that early Iberians were cannibals.

Cro-Magnon migration across the Pyrenees from France about 35,000 years ago, gave the Iberian Peninsula its first modern human inhabitants. Gradually, as their societies evolved and other peoples arrived from the north through migration and invasion, the Iberian Peninsula became a patchwork of competing territories, populated by peoples with distinct cultures and languages. By 6000BC agriculture and animal husbandry had arrived in the south, where Iberia's first fortified villages were built.

From about 800BC the **Phoenicians** (from the Eastern Mediterranean), **Greeks** and **Carthaginians** (from north Africa), began establishing colonies along the Mediterranean coast to facilitate trade with the interior. Although these colonies were small, their cultural influence spread throughout southern and eastern Iberia, fusing with local customs to create a distinctly Iberian culture, which built cities and developed writing systems based on the Phoenician and Greek alphabets.

This increased outside influence corresponded with the arrival of Celtic peoples from Gaul (G), who settled mostly in the north and west. There they built the characteristic round *Castro* settlements, the ruins of which can still be seen in parts of Galicia.

Outside political interference in the internal affairs of Iberia remained insignificant until the Carthaginians began, in the aftermath of the 1st **Punic War** (264BC to 241BC), to enlist Iberian tribes to fight on their side against the Romans.

ROMAN HISPANIA

It wasn't until 201BC, with the defeat of the Carthaginian by the Romans in the 2nd Punic War, that Rome gained control of the coast from the Pyrenees to the Algarve and began to play a greater role in the territory they named **Hispania**.

Unlike earlier colonists, Rome was interested in more than just trade, and set about consolidating its rule through the subjugation of the native peoples. Within two hundred years, through a combination of force, forging local alliances and exploiting enmities between native tribes, Rome had succeeded in imposing its will across most of Hispania and, although some scattered resistance continued, the foundations had been laid for the disappearance of the pre-Roman Iberian peoples and the dominance of Roman culture throughout the peninsula – the only exception being the Basques, whose culture and language persist to this day.

The Romans brought with them their language, religious practices, laws, governance, architecture and economic organisation. They integrated Hispania into the greater Roman world. Colonisation and the romanisation of the local ruling elite soon cemented this process. A network of roads was built which facilitated the movement of soldiers and gave local produce access to wider markets. Improved irrigation systems (some of which still functions today) and farming methods led to increases in agricultural production. Hispania became a major exporter of olive oil and wine as well as gold and silver from the mines of Asturias.

In time, Hispania began to play an important role in Roman history. It is the birth place of two of Rome's *Five Good Emperors* (G): **Trajan** (Emperor from 98 to 117), born in southern Hispania, is remembered for the many public buildings he commissioned in Rome, and **Hadrian** (Emperor from 117 to 138), born in **Italica** on the Vía de la Plata, who, besides his famous wall, also constructed the Temple of Venus and Roma in Rome.

Besides emperors, Hispania also gave Rome one of its greatest philosophers and statesmen, in the person of **Seneca the Younger** (4BC to 65AD), also born in southern Hispania.

At first the Roman settlers brought with them their traditional pantheon of deities, but following the conversion to **Christianity** of the Emperor Constantine I, some time before 337, the Roman Empire began to serve as a conduit for Christianity. However, despite the outlawing of polytheist practices in 392, it took several centuries before this new and foreign religion spread beyond the urban elite and began to achieve any success among the more traditional rural peoples.

The Roman period also marked the beginning of Jewish settlement in Hispania. Over the following centuries this Jewish community would become one of the most important in the world.

HISPANIA / IBERIA / ESPAÑA

Spain has had several different names through history. Pre-Roman Spain is generally referred to as **Iberia**, *a name which is still used today but which refers to the entire Iberian Peninsula (Spain, Portugal, Andorra and Gibraltar). The Romans named their Iberian territories* **Hispania**, *which also referred to the entire Iberian Peninsula. The modern words for* **Spain** *in various languages (España, Espagne, Spanien) all evolved from the Roman name Hispania.*

THE VISIGOTHS

Roman hegemony in Hispania remained unchallenged until the 4th century, when repercussions of events further to the north began to be felt south of the Pyrenees. The Germanic tribes of central and south-eastern Europe, who had long harried the frontiers of the Empire, began a westwards migration, prompted by pressure for territory and facilitated by weakness in Rome.

Starting around 400, the **Vandals** and **Alans**, nomadic Germanic tribes from the Caucasus, crossed the Pyrenees (possibly through Roncesvalles) and established short-lived kingdoms. They were followed a few years later by the **Visigoths**, who had been in Gaul (G) for some time and had adopted many Roman customs and traditions, including Christianity. The Visigoths established their capital in Toledo and quickly 'persuaded' the other Germanic tribes to move on to north Africa.

The Visigoths were to rule unchallenged over most of Hispania for the next 400 years. Under them life in Hispania changed little. Latin continued to be the language of administration and education, the supremacy of Roman law continued and Christianity slowly replaced traditional polytheist practices among the general population.

At the same time, important events were happening far to the east in Arabia which were to have a profound effect on the future of Hispania and the world. Around 570, **Muhammad ibn Abdullah** was born in the city of Mecca. He founded a monotheistic religion, **Islam**, which over the following centuries spread rapidly with the **Arab Empire** across western Asia and north Africa, challenging the predominance of Christianity there, and eventually also in parts of Europe.

The Arab Empire spread into the political vacuum left by the collapse of the Roman Empire around the eastern and southern shores of the Mediterranean, and created the social and political conditions which allowed Islam, over the course of the next centuries, to follow in its wake. By 630 the Arab Empire and its religion had reached Morocco, with the hills of Hispania tantalisingly visible across the Straits of Gibraltar.

Despite ruling Hispania, the Visigoths were fatally weakened by their own internal feuding. Around 711, it's alleged that an important Visigoth family, the Witizas, in an attempt to gain the upper hand in a power struggle with another family, summoned the aid of Berber tribes from North Africa who had recently converted to Islam. Thus began a sequence of events that would profoundly change the course of Spanish history.

AL-ANDALUS

In 711, an army led by **Tariq ibn-Ziyad** landed at Gibraltar and, meeting only ineffectual resistance from the divided Visigoths, succeeded over the next ten or so years in taking control of most of Hispania and advancing over the Pyrenees into southern Gaul, where their expansion temporarily faltered, before attaining its maximum extent by reaching Provence and Burgundy. Most of Hispania fell under Muslim control, whether direct or by proxy through the local Iberians or Visigoths nobility. Only a small strip of land along the north coast, protected by impenetrable mountains, remained outside their domain.

The Arabs called their new territories in Europe **Al-Andalus**, from which name comes the present-day **Andalusia**. They moved its capital from Toledo, which had been the Visigoth seat of government, first to Seville and later to Córdoba.

At first Al-Andalus was ruled by governors sent from Damascus or appointed by the Arab rulers of North Africa. However, from 740, a series of internal conflicts in Al-Andalus weakened outside control and allowed **Yusuf al-Fihri**, governor of Narbonne, to govern the territory as an independent entity until 756, when an exiled Syrian prince called **Abd-ar-Rahman I,** deposed al-Fihri and declared himself **Emir of Córdoba**. Over the next century and a half he and his successors ruled over Al-Andalus as an independent state, in defiance of the centralised control from Damascus.

In 929, one of his descendants, **Abd-ar-Rahman III**, proclaimed himself **Caliph of the Caliphate of Córdoba,** thus beginning a period of political unity which many regard as a golden era in the history of Muslim Spain.

SOCIETY IN DIVIDED SPAIN

The Muslim population of Al-Andalus was small at first but grew rapidly during the 200 years following the invasion, largely as a result of intermarriage and conversion. The majority of Muslim invaders were Berbers, who were discriminated against by the Arab ruling class. This factor was to be a constant source of tension and division within Al-Andalus.

For the first 300 years following the Muslim invasion, the different ethnic groups lived in close proximity to each other in a patchwork of semi-autonomous ghettos, their social and cultural lives kept separate by religious taboos and laws against intermarriage. While Christians and Jews were allowed a large degree of autonomy in running their own affairs, they were also considered second-class citizens and excluded from positions of power outside their own communities.

However, for the native population there were some benefits from Muslim rule. Taxes were lowered and those willing to convert to Islam were freed from vassalage. Jews, who had suffered discrimination under the Christian Visigoths, were now considered to be on the same level as them. The Jewish community prospered over the following centuries Al-Andalus, with a prosperous intelligentsia, became an important centre in the global Jewish community.

During this time, agriculture prospered thanks to new irrigation techniques and crops (rice and spinach). Great palaces and mosques were built (many of which are still standing and remarkably well-preserved), the city of Córdoba became the largest and most advanced in Europe, with a population of a quarter of a million people and extensive drinking water and sewage systems, as well as street lighting.

The Muslims also brought with them their advanced understanding of mathematics and astronomy. The first use of Arabic numerals, still in use today, by Europeans was recorded in Spain in the 10th century. The abacus appeared in Europe around the same time.

This exchange of ideas and technologies underlines the porous nature of the borders between the various kingdoms and caliphates. Individuals passed back and forth between the different areas with relative ease. The filtering of ideas north was helped by a small but significant flow of Christian migrants wishing to escape Muslim rule. These **Mozarabic**, or Arabised, Christians played a role in forming the unique hybrid culture which was developing throughout Hispania.

Linguistically the picture became equally diverse. In Al-Andalus, Arabic and Berber speakers rubbed shoulders with speakers of Latin languages, while in the north regional differences were leading to the development of distinct new languages, stemming from a common Latin root, in Galicia, Castile, Aragon and Catalonia. Meanwhile, Basque extended its territory southwards into central Navarra.

THE RECONQUISTA

The term **Reconquista**, means *reconquest.* It refers to a historical process which culminated in the re-establishment of Christian dominance in the Iberian Peninsula.

It is difficult to define an exact beginning, and for much of the Reconquista, it was far from obvious that it was a process at all, due to the sporadic and inconclusive nature of events, shifting alliances which were often motivated by political expediency rather than religious loyalties, and advances and retreats by both sides. However, it is sometimes considered to have begun early in the 8th century, when a rebellion against Muslim rule, led by a Visigoth nobleman called **Pelagius** (*Pelayo* in Spanish, not to be confused with Pelayo (See *History of the Camino*, page 106) the hermit), broke out in Asturias.

The origins of this rebellion are a little unclear, and it is possible that Pelagius' motivation was not the reinstatement of Visigoth power, or indeed the defence of Christianity, and that his establishment of a Christian kingdom in Asturias was an accidental consequence of an unplanned series of events which began with a disagreement between a Muslim governor, Munuza, and Pelagius over Pelagius' sister.

As is wont to happen when male pride is dented and the honour of a female relative is called into question, things quickly spiralled out of control. An army was raised to subdue the rebellious north led by the Muslim General Alkama, reputedly accompanied by the Visigoth Bishop of Seville, Oppa.

The historical facts relating to the subsequent **Battle of Covadonga** (722) are disputed, with some historians describing it as a mere skirmish. However, its real significance lies in that it was portrayed by the Christians as a great victory over the Muslims. It is sometimes even cited as the inspiration of the mythical **Battle of Clavijo**. Following this victory Pelagius ruled Asturias independently of the Muslims for nineteen years and was succeeded by his son Falfila.

Events outside Hispania, and the increasing involvement of foreigners in the Reconquista, were also important. At about this time a Muslim army suffered a serious military defeat at the hands of the Franks (G) near Toulouse. Then, in 777, **Charlemagne** (G), meeting with Muslim leaders who opposed the then Emir of Al-Andalus, hatched a plot with them to help in their struggle against the Emir. To this end he sent a force which besieged the city of Zaragoza, but failed to take it. Retreating through the Pyrenees, the rearguard of Charlemagne's army was ambushed and defeated in the **Battle of Roncesvalles**.

UNIFICATION AND TERRITORIAL ADVANCES

In 1072, having defeated his two brothers and rivals to the throne, **King Alfonso VI (el Bravo/the Brave, 1040 - 1109)**, succeeded in unifying the kingdoms of León, Galicia and Castile under his rule. He went on to become the first king to recapture a large amount of territory from the Muslims by advancing as far as Toledo, symbolic for being the ancient capital of the Visigoths. The different ethnic groups in the recaptured territories lived peacefully together under his rule. However, by 1086 a Muslim army strengthened by Berbers from a strict Muslim sect who had recently crossed from north Africa inflicted a defeat on him and went on to retake much of the territory he had previously recaptured.

Gradually, over the course of the next century, the Christian kingdoms again pushed their area of control southwards, taking Lisbon in 1147, with help from northern European crusaders and, briefly, Almeria, with the help of a fleet from Italy.

In 1212 a unified force from Navarra, Castile and Aragon defeated the Muslims in **Las Navas de Tolosa**, marking the beginning of a key phase of decline for Muslim rule in southern Spain. The Christian forces now advanced decisively, and Córdoba was taken in 1236. **King Fernando III of Castile (el Santo/the Saint, 1199 - 1252),** before entering the city, ordered that anyone who wished to leave was free to do so. Upon entering the city one of his first acts was to have the bells of Santiago cathedral removed from the Great Mosque, where they had been used as ornaments, and transported back to Santiago where space had been left for them in the cathedral which was rebuilt after its destruction by al-Mansur (G) in 997.

Thereafter Muslims controlled only the **Kingdom of Granada**.

Large Muslim and Jewish populations came under Christian rule as a result of the Reconquista. The Muslims were mostly farmers, whereas the Jews lived mostly in urban areas, practising trades and money-lending. At first they were allowed to continue to practise their religions as before. However, this was soon to change.

THE CATHOLIC MONARCHS AND THE FALL OF GRANADA

The marriage in 1469 of **Queen Isabel I of Castile (1451 - 1504)** and **King Fernando II of Aragon (1452 - 1516)** united two important kingdoms, Castile and Aragon, and marked the beginning of an important phase in Spanish history. Usually referred to as **The Catholic Monarchs (*Los Reyes Católicos*)**, they were believed by many of their subjects to have been sent by God to rid Spain of the Muslims. Queen Isabel was even sometimes referred to as a second Virgin Mary.

Once in power, they implemented a number of policies intended to build a strong, unified and centralised state. To this end they created the **Brotherhood (*La Hermandad*)**, to take control of the administration of justice and the waging of war on Granada. In order to create alliances with potential allies and rivals they married their children into other royal houses.

Over two hundred years since the fall of Córdoba, only Granada remained independent and under Muslim control, a thorn in the sides of Spain's Christian rulers. During these years, Granada's leaders concentrated on building fortified towns to defend the frontiers of their mountainous kingdom. Meanwhile, the Kingdom of Castile was developing its siege breaking abilities, with advances in the use of gunpowder and cannon. Both sides engaged in frequent raids into each others' territory, taking slaves and engaging in looting and destruction, while avoiding any large-scale confrontation.

This was a state-of-affairs that the Catholic Monarchs were not willing to allow to continue. To this end, they began a long and bloody military campaign, which culminated in the fall of Granada. It was a hard-fought campaign. The Muslims defended from their fortified towns, which the Christians, despite their heavy artillery, had great difficulty in taking.

Appeals for help by Granada to other Muslim states in North Africa and Western Asia, went unanswered, and in 1487, with the help of soldiers from Germany, England and France, Malaga fell after a three-month siege with many dead on both sides. Other defensive towns followed Malaga until finally, in the spring of 1490, the Christian forces were at the gates of Granada itself. Once there, doubtful of their ability to take the city's formidable defensive walls by force, they sat down and waited. They were still there 18 months later, in 1492, when secret negotiations secured a surrender on terms which were acceptable to both sides. Under this deal, Muslims were offered a large degree of freedom to practise their religion and culture.

Flushed from their victory over the Muslims, the Catholic Monarchs decided to expel all Jews from Spain. Around 160,000 members of this ancient community were scattered to the four winds. Only those who became Christians were allowed to stay. They are thought to have numbered around 200,000. The Jews of Spain had made up a large part of the country's intellectual and mercantile classes, and their departure was a great loss to Spanish society and to its economy.

In the years after 1492, many members of the Muslim ruling class also abandoned Spain for north Africa, and Granada ceased to be an important Muslim city. The rulers of Spain expected that the remaining Muslims, being mostly 'common folk', would quickly convert. When this didn't happen, despite financial incentives, the policy of tolerance changed to one of forced conversion, which led to an unsuccessful rebellion in 1499. The Muslims were then offered the choice of conversion or expulsion.

However, due to several factors, including a shortage of Arabic-speaking teachers and priests, forced conversion was never very successful. This left Spain with a large population of Arabic-speakers whose conversion to Christianity was often only superficial.

THE SPANISH INQUISITION

In 1478 the Catholic Monarchs obtained a Papal Bull from **Pope Sixtus IV,** setting up the **Spanish Inquisition**, along similar lines to Inquisitions in other countries, to enable them to deal with Jewish converts to Christianity, known as *conversos*, who were widely suspected of being insincere in their adaptation of Christianity since their conversion had been under duress.

The Spanish Inquisition had wide-ranging and arbitrary powers of arrest, trial and punishment, which were limited only by royal approval. Even the Pope was unable to question its decisions. It used these powers against those whom it considered to be enemies of Catholicism. All agents of the Inquisition were appointed by, and hence loyal to, the crown. It operated in secret and had an army of informers. The accused had no right to legal representation or even to question the accusations made against them. The use of torture to extract confessions was common. It could, and frequently did, confiscate the property of the accused, even using it to reward their accusers.

In its early years most of its victims were *conversos*, of whom several thousand were convicted and burned at the stake, a fate which many more escaped only by fleeing the country. The public sentencing and punishment of its unfortunate victims became popular spectacles with the general population.

After the expulsion of the Jews and Muslims, the Inquisition found a new lease of life in policing the religious lives of ordinary Spaniards with special attention paid to their sexual activities. Its operation, together with the centralising impulse started by Fernando and Isabel, made Spain a blueprint for modern totalitarian regimes.

The Inquisition continued to act as a totalitarian control on the cultural and intellectual life of Spain until its abolition in 1834. Furthermore, it changed the role of Roman Catholicism from a mere religion to that of a state ideology, loyalty to which was equated with loyalty to the crown. This placed the Church centre-stage in Spanish politics, playing an active and partisan role in the events and conflicts to come.

1492

Fourteen-ninety-two was a momentous year in Spanish and world history, not just because of events in Spain itself, but also because it was the year of the 'discovery' of the Americas by Christopher Columbus, in an expedition partly funded by the Spanish crown. This led to a period of extraordinary imperial expansion which made Spain the centre of the first global empire and allowed it to accumulate massive wealth which made it, for several centuries, the world's pre-eminent seafaring power. At different times over the next four hundred years, that empire covered much of North and South America, northern and southern Morocco, the Philippines and many small territories on the coasts of Africa and Asia, stretching as far as China. It spread Spanish language, culture and the Roman Catholic religion far and wide, transforming forever the societies of much of the Americas and the Philippines. In Central and South America, Spanish conquistadores (G) encountered civilisations with advanced social and economic organisation. None, however, was able to resist long against the weapons, cunning and communicable diseases which the Spanish brought with them. Great riches in the form of precious metals were brought back to Spain, by 1590 three million kilograms of silver was arriving every year, helping to fund magnificent building projects in Spanish cities and towns and (mostly futile) attempts to extend Spanish power in Europe.

SPAIN UNDER THE HAPSBURGS

When **Fernando** died in 1516 the Spanish throne passed to his son **Carlos I de España (1500 – 1558)** who was already serving as King of the Netherlands and was a **Hapsburg (G)**. The succession was not without its difficulties, but Carlos eventually established his authority as **King of Castile,** while at the same time becoming **Emperor of the Holy Roman Empire** and ruler of a territory that covered much of western and central Europe. Under his rule Spain came to play an increasingly important role in the running of the empire, providing many of its soldiers and much of its tax revenue.

Felipe II (el Prudente / the Prudent, 1527 - 1598) succeeded Carlos in 1556, lost Germany in the process but managing to keep control of much of Italy, the Netherlands, Belgium and Luxembourg. Felipe was married to **Queen Mary I of England (Bloody Mary, 1516 – 1558)** and so was co-monarch of England until her death. He moved his court to **Madrid** in 1561, favouring its central location over Seville.

Despite their lost political power, the Muslim population in **Andalusia** (as Al-Andalus was now called) was still separated by religion, language and culture from the rest of Spain, and Felipe was keen to enforce religious and cultural uniformity. When, in 1567, the government in Madrid began to enforce a policy of forbidding the use of Arabic and the wearing of Arab clothes as well as traditional singing and dancing, this and other punitive measures resulted in an uprising know in Spanish as **La Rebelión de las Alpujarras.**

A year of fruitless negotiations preceded the uprising in Las Alpujarras, a mountainous region south of Granada. Once started it soon turned into all-out war between Muslim rebels and the royal army. In this final conflict the Muslims, with their backs to the wall, and possibly sensing what was to come, fought to the last, with appalling atrocities committed by both sides against civilians and combatants. The uprising lasted two years and resulted in the final crushing of Muslim resistance, and the deportation of the remaining Muslim populations and their resettlement in remote parts of Castile. The revolt had cost many thousands of lives on both sides.

In 1599 the **Plague** (G) arrived in Spain and killed half a million people. Urban dwellers and monastic communities were worst affected because the disease could spread more easily among people living in close quarters.

A long-running debate about what to do about the **Moriscos** (G) came to a head in 1609. Morisco is the term used to describe people who had been forced to convert from Islam to Christianity, many of whom continued to practise Islam in secret. Extremists wanted the Moriscos expelled while moderates argued for more time and resources to complete their absorption into the Christian church. The extremists, many of whom stood to gain financially from expelling the Moriscos, won the debate and 260,000 Moriscos were forced to leave Spain, mostly for north Africa, where their descendants still live, losing in the process the lands they had worked for centuries.

Felipe's reign over the rest of his empire was also not without incident. It was a crucial time in the **Reformation,** when different religious groups were competing for power in Europe's patchwork of states. In an effort to dissuade the English from assisting Protestant rebels in the Netherlands, he launched the ill-judged and, eventually disastrous, invasion attempt which became known in English as the **Spanish Armada**. The Armada suffered an early defeat while anchored off the south coast of England, and only managed to escape English forces by sailing through the English Channel, with the intention of returning to Spain via a circuitous route over the top of Scotland. The vicious north Atlantic weather was its undoing, and off the west of Ireland it encountered severe gales which wrecked many ships. Of the ships that set sail from Spain only around half returned.

Poor leadership in this period contributed greatly to Spain's loss of influence around Europe. The Thirty Years' War against the Netherlands bankrupted and exhausted Castile. Revolts in Portugal and Catalonia only made things worse, and led to the definitive loss of Portugal. Economic mismanagement led to its currency losing value. Unrest continued with revolutions in Spain's Italian territories.

The **Thirty Years' War** involved all the great powers in Europe and laid waste to much of the continent. Its origins lay in the conflict between Catholic and Protestant areas of the **Holy Roman Empire,** but as it progressed it became more about power politics between warring royal families, especially the Hapsburgs and the Bourbons. It caused enormous economic difficulties for Castile and a fall in population from 8.5 million to 6.6 million, which was only partially compensated for by immigration from France. Despite managing to minimise its territorial losses, Spain's position as the dominant power in Europe was greatly undermined, causing France to launch a series of attacks against Spanish possessions in the Low Countries.

SPAIN UNDER THE BOURBONS

In 1700, the rule of the Hapsburgs came to an end when **Carlos II (el Hechizado / the Bewitched, 1661 – 1700)** died leaving no heir. He did however, leave a will bequeathing the throne to a relative of King Louis XIV of France, thus essentially handing Spain to the Bourbon (G) royal family. In response, both England and Austria invaded Spain.

The ensuing war was won by the new **Bourbon King Felipe V**, but at the cost of the loss of Spain's possessions in Europe. Bourbon rule continued for all of the 1700s, while Spain's economy experienced sluggish growth helped by trade with the Americas and hindered by mismanagement and conservatism.

The **French revolution** overthrew Bourbon rule in France, leading Spain to declare war on the revolutionary government following the execution of Louis XVI in 1793. The following year the French invaded Spain, overwhelming the Spanish who quickly sued for peace. The peace was not to last however, and in 1808 the French invaded again and forced **King Carlos IV (1748 - 1819)** to abdicate.

Spanish independence was won again largely thanks to Irishman Arthur Wellesley (later to become the **Duke of Wellington** (G)), who, in a campaign known as the **War of Independence** in Spain and the **Peninsular Wars** in Britain, advanced from Portugal at the head of a British army assisted by Spanish and Portuguese forces, and defeated the French at Salamanca in 1812 and at Vitoria in 1813.

In the aftermath of the war, with **Fernando VII (el Deseado / the Desired, 1784 – 1833)** imprisoned in France, the group which had governed the country in his absence assembled a **Cortes** (parliament) to draw up a constitution, often referred to as the **Constitution of Cadiz**, which foresaw the establishment of a parliament to limit the powers of the monarchy, and many other innovations in state administration, many inspired by revolutionary France. After his return however, Fernando quickly re-established himself as absolute leader.

This brief flirtation with devolved power sowed the seeds for many more, often short-lived, experiments in more-or-less democratic power-sharing, which were always followed by virulent counter-measures from the monarchist side. This to-ing and fro-ing continued throughout the 19th century and into the 20th. This meant, in practice, frequent revolts, revolutions and counter-revolutions, with different factions running the country at different times.

Eventually, a revolution in 1868 led to the introduction of **universal male suffrage**, **freedom of religion** and the establishment of a **republic** in 1873.

Other developments during the 19th century were the increasing interventionism of the army in the country's political life, sometimes on the side of reform and sometimes on the side of the monarchy, and the influence that political ideologies such as **republicanism, fascism, Marxism** and **anarchism** began to have on Spanish politics. It also saw the loss of Spain's last colonial possessions in the Americas and Europe.

SPAIN IN THE 20TH CENTURY

The dawn of the 20th century saw Spain being ruled by a monarchy with some elements of power-sharing. Catalan and Basque nationalist movements were active, and were opposed by elements both in the political class and in the army. Republicanism was gathering strength and anarchism was spreading its influence through the labour movement. Anarchists opposed political organisation, relying instead on direct action by workers, to challenge employers and the ruling class directly.

An attempt to call up reservists to the army led to the calling of a general strike in Barcelona on 26 July 1909, in what became known as the **Barcelona Revolt**. Thousands of workers responded by pouring onto the streets and erecting barricades. The security forces rapidly lost control of the city and violence and looting was widespread, with anarchists and their supporters burning churches and monasteries.

Security forces counter-attacked and, within a few days, the government had retaken the city. The success of the general strike and the ease with which workers, albeit briefly, had taken control, emboldened the working class and precipitated the establishment of the **CNT** (*National Confederation of Labour / Confederación Nacional del Trabajo*) as an amalgamation of all the existing anarchist and libertarian unions.

The anarchists increased their power during **World War I,** when real wages fell and the membership of the CNT increased. Simultaneously, a faction dedicated to the use of violence developed within the CNT, which the leadership could not control.

A strike in Barcelona in 1919 was the biggest to date. The response to it by the employers, and their use of violence and assassination to defeat the strikers, only served to further radicalise the working class.

A palace coup now brought to power a dictator, **Primo de Rivera**, committed to handing power over to civilian leaders. He ruled with the support of the army and the king, but his failure to gain popular support for his plans for the country, and his (very mild) attacks on army privileges, soon put an end to his army support. In 1931, after local elections showed strong support for republicanism, the king, fearing civil war, left Spain and the Second Republic was founded.

The **Second Republic** was an attempt to reconcile Spain's increasingly extreme political groups, of the left and right, through democracy. It wasn't particularly successful. Left and right-wing governments succeeded each other in rapid succession, while industrial and agrarian unrest continued, causing the extremist elements on each side to grow in strength and belligerence. By 1936 the stage was set for the violent show-down that would define Spanish politics for the rest of the century and beyond.

THE CIVIL WAR

The elections of early 1936 were marred by violence, most of it originating in the nationalist **Falange Party**. When the left-wing, republican **Popular Front** emerged as the winner by a slim margin, the street violence continued and the Falange began to appeal to the army to save 'Spain from Marxism'.

The army revolt against the government, in which **General Francisco Franco** played a key role, began in the Spanish protectorate of Northern Morocco, in July 1936, and quickly spread to the mainland, where the revolt achieved only partial success due to the resistance of workers and security forces opposed to the army. This left Spain divided, with the republicans controlling Madrid, Catalonia, the Basque Country and the Mediterranean coast, and the Nationalists controlling the south, the rural centre and Galicia.

The republicans were supported by the Soviet Union, Mexico and the international labour movement. They also received the support of many thousands of volunteers from all over the world who joined the **International Brigade** to fight fascism.

Although the **Nationalists' ideology** was markedly different from fascism, venerating the Mother Church rather than any notions about racial purity, they received the support of **Nazi Germany** and **Fascist Italy,** who regarded them more as allies against communism than ideological bedfellows. They also received the help of many thousands of volunteers motivated by a desire to protect Roman Catholicism from the 'red menace'. Some of these volunteers were really military aid in disguise, as in the case of the Italians, who sent a significant number of troops in this way. Others were incompetent to the point of being a liability, such as the Irish, most of whose casualties resulted from a skirmish with their own side, and the twin distractions of dusky Spanish women and an abundance of cheap wine.

In many Republican areas, *de facto* power lay in the hands of the workers' committees, rather than the democratically elected government, and they set about implementing a series of socialist policies, such as nationalisation of industry and collectivisation of agricultural land. At the same time, the membership and influence of the Communist Party grew rapidly, due to its control of the flow of arms from the Soviet Union, of crucial importance because of the refusal of Britain and France to allow the republican government to buy arms from other sources.

The civil war might have ended quickly if Franco's advance hadn't been stopped by stiffer-than-expected resistance in Madrid, where the militias and the **International Brigade** succeeded in mounting an effective defence of the city.

This setback was only temporary, and ultimately the Nationalists won the war because they had a disciplined, professional core to their army, based on General Franco's Africa Army, and from 1936 onwards they were united politically under Franco. They also had more help from outside Spain, with Italy sending 70,000 soldiers and Germany sending a fleet of 100 aircraft. Both also sent tanks and artillery.

By contract, the Republican army was mostly made up of poorly trained and lightly armed volunteers, and their political leadership was deeply divided along ideological lines with conflict between **Stalinist**, **Trotskyite** and **anarchist** factions sometimes erupting into violence. Its main arms supplies came from the Soviet Union and included tanks, aircraft and artillery. However, after 1938 these supplies stopped as the Soviet Union began preparations for a Nazi invasion.

The Nationalist side used terror against its opponents in a systematic and deliberate manner, in the areas it occupied. During the war at least 80,000 people were killed for political reasons by the Nationalist side, away from the battlefields.

On the Republican side there were also numerous political killings, including around 7,000 clergy. However, most killings took place early in the war, before the government had had the opportunity to assert its authority, and lacked the element of tactical deliberation present on the Nationalist side.

The killing of clergy is often attributed to anti-clericalism, and without a doubt there was some element of that involved. However, the Roman Catholic Church, internationally and locally, was strongly politically engaged on the Nationalist side during the Civil War and so was regarded by many on the Republican side as a combatant.

The bombing of the Basque town **Guernica / Gernika** in 1937, by German aircraft, shocked and outraged international public opinion. It was the first time the world had witnessed the military tactics that would later become known as **Blitzkrieg** and that would allow Nazi armies to overrun much of Europe.

The civil war ended in 1939, when the Nationalists entered Madrid and Barcelona. The war had lasted three years and, although no exact figure is known, certainly cost the lives of several hundred thousand people. As with all civil wars, it left a legacy of bitter division through families and communities that was to last for generations.

SPAIN UNDER FRANCO

Exhausted by its civil war, Spain stayed officially neutral in **World War II**, although it did send 50,000 troops to fight with the Nazis against the USSR in the *Blue Division / División Azul*. However, Franco's enthusiasm for the Nazi cause waned somewhat as the outcome of the war became clear.

The Spanish economy suffered from the destruction of infrastructure and disruption of economic activity caused by the civil war, and living standards dropped back to levels similar to those seen fifty years earlier.

In the post-war years, opposition to Franco's regime was sporadic. One serious attempt was made in the 1950s to re-instate the monarchy, but it petered out due to opposition from some factions within the regime (the Carlists) to a Bourbon monarchy, and Franco's promise that he would prepare the ground for a return to monarchy after his death.

The regime's hand was strengthened by its effective playing of the anti-Communist card, leading to an agreement with the United States to grant it financial aid in return for allowing the establishment of US military bases on Spanish territory. Despite this, NATO membership did not come until after democracy was restored.

Although the regime was firmly entrenched, its economic problems continued. Franco's policies of economic self-sufficiency and protectionism for state-owned industries, left the economy with little potential for growth. In the late 1950s changes in these policies, partly under the guidance of Opus Dei (G) ministers in the government, led to less interventionism and opening to foreign trade and capital investment. These policies produced a spurt of rapid economic growth during the 1960s, causing the country to modernise rapidly, with employment in agriculture falling and mass migration from rural areas to cities, where industrial jobs were available. This period also saw large-scale emigration to other European countries, especially France, Switzerland and Germany.

The Roman Catholic hierarchy supported the regime, but many younger priests, under the influence of Vatican II and the radicalising effects of service in poor countries, were supportive of the democratic movement.

Periodic resistance continued from students and unofficial strikes by workers. In the Basque Country *Euskadi Ta Askatsuna* (**ETA**) continued its campaign of violent resistance to the regime and in favour of Basque independence. It scored a direct hit in 1973 with the assassination of **Carrero Blanco**, who had just become Franco's prime minister and who had been tipped to succeed him.

DEMOCRATIC SPAIN

In 1975, Franco died and **King Juan Carlos** became head of state. The following year the Cortes passed the **Law for Political Reform,** which paved the way for the democratic elections of 1977. The *Unión de Centro Democrático* (**UCD**) led by an ex-Francoist minister, **Adolpho Suárez González**, running on a consensus platform, became the biggest party. The UDC government gave Spain its current constitution in 1978, establishing it as a constitutional monarchy and granting vaguely worded compromises on autonomy to the regions. However, in-fighting and economic problems led to Suárez's resignation in 1981.

The transfer of power to the new UDC leader was interrupted by a **coup attempt** by Lieutenant Colonel Antonio Tejero, who occupied the Cortes and held the deputies at gun point for 18 hours. The coup was only patchily supported inside the army, and King Juan Carlos' television appearance pledging his support for democracy swung waverers in favour of the government and gained the king a personal popularity which ensured the continuance of constitutional monarchy.

The elections in 1982 saw the *Partido Socialista Obrero Español / Spanish Socialist Workers Party* (**PSOE**) emerge as clear winners with **Felipe González** at its head. His government made controlling inflation and modernising Spain's economy its priorities. It also held a referendum on **NATO membership,** which passed, and steered Spain successfully into the **EEC** (European Economic Community, which subsequently became the **European Union**).

This period coincided with a rush of creativity and social change which became known as **La Movida** (*The Movement*). Spain's Gay and Lesbian communities, which had previously been the targets of repressive legislation, were suddenly able to live in the open, at least in the big cities. Women also acquired much greater freedom, with the breaking of social taboos and discrimination which had previously confined them to their traditional roles as mothers and housewives. Economic expansion, which accompanied Spain's membership of the EU, offered women a degree of personal freedom which they had never had before. Greater availability of contraception and abortion, freed women from the fear of back-street abortions. EU membership also gave young people opportunities to travel and study abroad.

During the 1980s, unemployment rose above 20%, provoking conflict with the hard-left and the trade unions in opposition to the government's pragmatic policies of withholding subsidies to unprofitable industries. However, the PSOE government was able to weather these storms and remain in power for four terms until 1996.

The *Partido Popular* (**PP**) won the elections of 1996 by a narrow margin, bringing to power **José María Aznar** in a coalition government supported by Basque and Catalan moderate nationalists. His government continued many of the economic policies the PSOE had pursued, while effecting deeper cuts in public spending. It was helped by a generally favourable economic climate during the 1990s, and was able to secure Spain's inclusion in the first wave of countries to join the EU's single currency, the euro, in 1999.

The PP won a landslide electoral victory in 2000, which allowed it to govern without the regional parties. The events of 11 September 2001, and the subsequent invasion of Iraq, which the PP supported enthusiastically, caused deep and bitter division in Spain, with the vast majority of the population opposing Spain's involvement in the war.

When, three days before the general election of 2004, ten bombs exploded on trains in Madrid, killing 191 people (an event known as **11-M**, 11 March, in Spanish), the PP immediately blamed ETA, and rushed the **UN Security Council** into issuing a declaration condemning ETA for the attacks. However, evidence emerged within days suggesting an Islamic extremist link to the attacks. With the clock counting down to the opening of voting, Spain lived through its tensest hours since the attempted coup of 1981, with rumours circulating among a frightened population of the army taking advantage of the situation to overthrow democracy.

Against all expectations the PSOE, under **José Luis Rodríguez Zapatero**, won the elections. Their victory was attributed to a reaction against the PP's impulsive reaction to the terrorist attacks. The rumours of an army takeover turned out to be just rumours and Spanish democracy came out of the experience strengthened, with the handover to the new government going without a hitch.

One of the new government's first acts was to announce a date for the withdrawal of the Spanish contingent in the occupying forces in Iraq, thus incurring the wrath of the then US president **George W Bush**.

The government went on to introduce a series of progressive social measures which challenged Spain's image as a conservative Catholic society. Educational reforms were introduced which were strongly opposed by both the PP and the Catholic Church. Spain became one of the first countries in Europe to introduce same-sex marriage and it has legislated and campaigned vigorously on the issue of violence against women.

Spain today

Spain is a constitutional monarchy and its head of state is **King Juan Carlos I de Borbón**. It has a bicameral parliament, the *Cortes Generales*, made up of the *Congreso de los Diputados*, elected by popular vote for a four-year term, and the *Senado*, elected partly by popular vote and partly appointed by the regions, also for a four-year term. Its Prime Minister, known as the *Presidente del Gobierno* / **President of the Government**, is **Mariano Rajoy Brey** of the conservative *Partido Popular* (PP).

On 1 January 2013, Spain had a population of 47,059,533 people. This is a decrease from 47,265,321 a year earlier, the first decrease in recent years, caused mostly by a decrease in the number of immigrants.

There were 5.5 million foreigners, down from 5.8 million two years earlier. They make up 11.7% of the population, the most numerous were (in descending order) Romanian, Moroccan, British, Ecuadorian and Colombian.

Life expectancy was 80.05 years, 83.57 for women and 76.74 for men.

"LA CRISIS"

The world economic crisis, triggered by the failure of regulation in the world financial system, took the **PSOE** government by surprise, and their late reaction delayed the implementation of measures to shore up Spain's banks and implement reforms in its economy.

In the **general elections of 2011** the **PP** won an outright majority. Their control of national government and most regional governments put them in a strong position to push through their policies. However, the depth and range of Spain's economic problems have severely limited their room to manoeuvre.

UNEMPLOYMENT

At 22.7% in May 2015, Spain's unemployment rate has dropped from a peak of 26% in 2012. At that date 3.57% more people were in employment than a year earlier. However, Spain remains second only to Greece in the EU for unemployment.

Youth unemployment is still a shade under 50% and falling slowly. Spanish people have adapted to survive. Emigration to Northern Europe and South America has increased, while other people have returned to subsistence farming in the villages their parents left in the 1960s and 1970s, for factory jobs in the cities.

The Spanish state provides some financial assistance to the unemployed. *Unemployment Benefit (Prestación contributiva)* is paid to persons who were made redundant, and had made a sufficient number of social security contributions while they were working. It's calculated at 70% of the person's last salary for six months, after which it reduces to 50%. It's normally paid for one third of the length of time that the person contributed. It's subject to a minimum and a maximum payment, depending on how many child dependants there are.

When Unemployment Benefit runs out, the state provides *Unemployment Assistance (Subsidio de desempleo)*. Receipt of this payment is subject to certain criteria, such as, having been made redundant, being over a certain age, having dependants, the income of the household, etc. The amount paid is 426,01€ per month.

NATIONALISM

ETA's (G) 2010 ceasefire has held in the Basque Country although an independence referendum seems to be off the agenda there for now.

Catalonia's government (*La Generalitat*) is also run by nationalist parties. There the economic crisis has increased calls for greater autonomy, with Catalonia's relative prosperity compared with the rest of Spain, transfers of tax to poorer regions, and Madrid's mismanagement of the economy, all cited as justifications for more autonomy. Although Spain's Constitutional Court ruled against allowing an independence referendum, the *Generalitat* organised an informal one which returned a large majority of Catalans in favour of independence. However, the process has no legal standing and was boycotted by many opponents of independence.

CURRENT EVENTS

Troublesome nationalists is only one of the problems facing Spain's current PP government led by Santiago-born **Mariano Rajoy Brey**. Years of dodgy accounting, secret payments to party apparatchiks, and multi-million euro Swiss bank accounts, have emerged from the obscure undergrowth of PP party politics to cause great discomfort for the government.

On the economic front, the government has concentrated its efforts on containing Spain's banking crisis, while introducing some reforms to liberalise the labour market. While taxes have risen, the minimum wage for those in unskilled employment has remained the same for a number of years at 645,30€ a month.

The emergency in 2014 of new political parties on both the left (*Podemos*) and right (*Ciudadanos*) of the political spectrum and their successes in European Parliament and local elections, was a clear sign of voters' discontent with the traditional parties and their links to cronyism and corruption. The electoral success of both parties has forced the established parties to negotiate with them to form coalitions in several regional assemblies.

Although the country's immediate future looks bleak, there is some reason for optimism from a booming tourism sector, strong growth in exports and the continuing strength of Spain's multinational businesses.

History of the Camino

EARLIEST EVIDENCE

The first written evidence linking St James the Great with Spain dates from the 6th or 7th century, when a Greek document of unknown origins, entitled *Breviarium Apostolorum*, gives an account of St James proselytising there during his lifetime. Other records, dating from around the 7th century, state that the Church of St Mary in Mérida possessed relics of St James and other apostles which were moved to an unspecified location in the North of Spain to escape the Muslim invasion.

Two hundred years later, a document called the *Martyrology of Usuard*, written by a French Benedictine monk **Usuard**, on his return from a journey to Galicia, describes the transportation of St James' relics from Jerusalem to Galicia.

Some earlier sources claim that the shrine in Santiago was the site of a burial ground, believed to contain the remains of another Christian martyr, **Priscillian of Avila** (G), who became the first Christian to be martyred by a Christian Roman Emperor when he was put to death by **Magnus Maximus** in 385. His remains are reputed to have been transported from Astorga to Santiago, along a route similar to the modern Camino Francés. Some people consider this to be the root of the tradition of pilgrimage to Santiago and claim that the relics in Santiago Cathedral are in fact those of Priscillian.

None of the early evidence supports the legend that the route of the Camino de Santiago, or any similar route, existed as a Roman or Druidic pilgrimage prior to the arrival of Christianity. However, given Christianity's habit of basing its feast days and holy places on pre-existing ones, it would hardly be surprising if the same had happened in this case.

CONTEXT OF THE DISCOVERY

The legend of St James was born at an opportune time in the history of Christianity in Spain. With the defeat of Charlemagne's (G) campaign to free Spain from Muslim domination in 778, and his retreat over the Puerto de Ibañeta pursued by Basque bandits, the divided and weak Christian kingdoms of the north were reduced to ruling over a narrow strip of mountainous land, geographically remote from the rest of Europe. Their prospects for resisting Muslim conquest must have seemed bleak, given how Islam had spread so rapidly, and appeared unstoppable. The momentum provided by the victory at the Battle of Covadonga and other successes against the Muslims, provided some slender grounds for optimism.

It was at this crucial moment in history that the legend of St James' connection to Spain began to spread through Europe with the discovery of his alleged burial site in **Iria Flavia** (near present-day *El Padrón*) in Christendom's most isolated and inaccessible western reaches, Galicia.

This event, its exact date is disputed but it is believed to lie between 788 and 838, was to have far-reaching consequences, and would transform this previously unremarkable region into a site of Christian pilgrimage second in Europe only to Rome, whose population - over a million at the height of the Roman Empire - had declined to about 30,000.

Crucially, it also provided a rallying and unifying impetus to the struggle against Muslim rule in Spain.

There are several versions of the legend of how St James' body came from Palestine to Galicia, but they all involve a boat which guided itself, and which brought St James' body, possibly accompanied by his two disciples, from Jaffa to either Provence, or straight to Galicia. In some accounts this boat is made of wood and in others it is made of stone.

THE DISCOVERY

There was, at that time, a hermit called **Pelayo** living in **Solovio** in the forest of **Libredón**, who dedicated his time to prayer and contemplation, surviving by a little fishing, hunting and scavenging. Palayo's peaceable existence was disturbed when he observed on several consecutive nights, what appeared to be stars falling from the sky. Convinced that this was a message of some sort, Pelayo paid a visit to his local bishop to ask his advice. **Bishop Teodomiro**, after consulting with his advisers and fasting for three days, went to the spot to see for himself and, impressed by what he saw, ordered a search of the place where the stars appeared to be falling. There he discovered, obscured by dense vegetation, a Roman chapel and burial ground, containing what he surmised to be the bodies of St James, two of his disciples, **Teodoro** and **Atanasio** and (according to some accounts) parchments or papyrus telling how they came to be there.

When **King Alfonso II of Asturias** heard of this, he quickly came to see for himself, following the Roman road from Oviedo to Santiago which is now known as the **Camino Primitivo** (page 79), thus becoming the first recorded pilgrim to Compostela. Satisfied with the relic's authenticity (and possibly also of their political usefulness), the King gave the discovery his royal approval, and had a small chapel built near the site.

News of the discovery spread quickly through Spain, Europe and beyond. It was important news that Europe now had a second apostolic shrine to rival Rome. Almost immediately pilgrims began to arrive, first from other regions of Spain, then France and later from further afield.

In the early days most of them travelled along the more secure northerly coastal routes, on what we now call the Camino del Norte and Camino Primitivo. It was only in the following centuries that gradual territorial advances against the Muslims led to the opening of the Meseta (G) route, which soon became known as the **Iter Francorum,** because of the number of Franks (G) who walked it and settled along it. This is what we now call the **Camino Francés**. This route quickly became the most popular with pilgrims because, being mostly flat, it was easier to walk. Quickly the Camino Francés became Northern Spain's main commercial artery, while the consequent strengthening of commercial ties with the rest of Europe brought an inflow of capital.

In the 11th century, **King Alfonso VI of Castile** emerged victorious in the struggle with his brothers for control of Galicia and Castile, and later extended his rule over Navarra and La Rioja, bringing for the first time most of Christian Spain together under one ruler. With Alfonso's encouragement, tolls and duty payments were eliminated for pilgrims, and a network of new monasteries was built by the Cistercian, Augustinian and Premonstratensian orders, under the control of the **Monastery of Cluny** (G) in eastern France. This began a period of extensive building along the Camino Francés, which lasted most of the 12th century, the results of which are still visible today. These new monasteries, hostels and churches provided a support infrastructure of accommodation, sustenance and care for pilgrims travelling to and from Santiago.

The 11th and 12th century were a time of population growth in Europe, partly due to a long period of mild weather, and France, with an estimated population of 18 to 20 million by 1328, was suffering from a shortage of agricultural land. This made the prospect of settling in underpopulated northern Spain quite attractive for many pilgrims.

THE ROLES OF CLUNY AND POPE CALIXTUS II

Cluniac influence led to the reform of Monastic life according to the new Franco-Papal norms. Liturgical uniformity was enforced, replacing the ancient and cherished **Mozarabic** (G) rites, and a new code of Canon Law was introduced. In secular life, new influences from the north also led to the introduction of social trends which changed the customs and mores of the ruling classes.

The triumvirate relationship between **Pope Calixtus II** (G), **Archbishop Gelmírez of Santiago** and **King Alfonso VI,** also played an important role in establishing Santiago de Compostela's status within the Church's hierarchy of religious sites. Pope Calixtus was related by marriage to Alfonso, and known to Gelmírez from the court of Aquitaine. During his papacy he lavished Santiago with funding and privileges, among them the power to grant indulgences (G) and the establishment of Holy Years.

He inspired the **Codex Calixtinus** (G), the first guide to the Camino. Probably compiled in Cluny and the work of several authors. It is in the form of an illustrated manuscript, with a detailed account of St James' life and a practical guide to travelling to his tomb, with descriptions of the towns and villages passed through, and the peoples living there.

Meantime, the numbers of pilgrims increased steadily, helped by the improved infrastructure of monasteries, hostels, roads and bridges. This steady flow of humanity in both directions became a conduit for the exchange of culture, ideas and technologies. New building techniques and architectural traditions were introduced into Spain, as well as the popular culture of the time; **storytelling, poetry, song** and **music**. The **Visigothic Script** was gradually replaced by the **Carolingian Minuscule** of France.

These developments were symptomatic of the general tendency of long distance pilgrimage to promote cultural exchange between societies, and uniformity and unity within the Church. This was a 'boom time' for pilgrimages generally, driven principally by a belief in the power of sacred relics to perform miracles and grant indulgences (G). Rome, Jerusalem, Santiago, Loreto, Mariazell and Canterbury, among others, competed for pilgrims.

The destruction of the cathedral in Santiago by **al-Mansur** (G) in 997, had cleared the way for the construction of the building which, in a much modified state, exists to this day. This grandiose building gave Santiago, by the end of the 12th century, a monument on a scale which rivalled anything in Rome, or any other pilgrimage site in Christendom.

Furthermore, with Jerusalem difficult to reach due to the political situation, only Rome and Santiago could offer pilgrims apostolic relics.

THE CRUSADES

In 1095 the first Crusade set out from Europe to attempt to free the **Holy Lands** from Muslim rule. This happened in the context of an outbreak of intense religious piety in Europe, partially cause by conflict between the ecclesiastical and civil authorities, and the growth in popularity of the notion of holy war against the enemies of the Church. Thanks to the growing popularity of Santiago as a pilgrimage site, the Church, led by Cluny and the papacy, was able to forge a link between the reconquest of Spain and the Crusades, and encourage outside involvement in the **Reconquista** through the participation of knights from other parts of Europe. By the time **Jerusalem** was captured in 1099, many ordinary Christians and their leaders had come to regard the Crusades and the Reconquista as being one and the same.

DECLINE

In the 14th century, the popularity of the Camino, and of pilgrimage in general, began to decline, due to a number of factors. The **Great Famine** of the early 14th century, caused by persistent heavy rain and crop failures in the spring and summer of 1315, killed millions and brought to an end a long period of population growth. The **Hundred Year War** between England and France, which lasted from the mid-14th to the mid-15th century and was fought largely on French territory, made travel in affected areas hazardous. The **Plague** (G) further reduced Europe's population in the mid-14th century, in places by as much as 50%, and caused a great fear of contact with strangers. It particularly devastated towns and monastic communities because it could spread more easily in places where people lived in close quarters.

Anti-pilgrim sentiment became common in the Church and society, partly as a consequence of the Plague, but also due to the number of **criminals** disguising themselves as pilgrims. As a result, the Church began to portray pilgrims as malingerers, who were avoiding their familial responsibilities by going on pilgrimages and wasting money which could be given to the local clergy. The veracity of relics was questioned, as was the point of travelling to a 'holy place' when Christianity taught of the omnipresence of God.

In the 15th century these criticisms became stronger, and many territories forbade pilgrimages which took longer than one day or involved crossing certain frontiers. Throughout Europe local pilgrimage sites were promoted by the Church as an alternative to more distant ones.

THE REFORMATION

The Reformation, which began in 1517, further reduced the number of potential pilgrims by banning pilgrimage outright. This led to a decline in long-distance pilgrimage, although it was not always successful in stopping much-loved practices which had deep roots in the community. The **Council of Trent** (G), set up by the Catholic Church to counter the claims of the Reformation, issued a number of decrees reaffirming practices which the Reformation rejected, such as **indulgences** (G), the **veneration of relics** and **pilgrimages**, while at the same time condemning abuses such as the sale of indulgences. In the case of pilgrimages the council was careful to specify that they should not be an excuse for gluttony and drunken excess (*ad commessationes et ebrietates*) or, debauchery and licentiousness (*per luxum ac lasciviam agentur*).

These conflicting attitudes to pilgrimage led to it becoming a badge of identity for Catholics and sometimes also a source of conflict with their Protestant neighbours, especially when it involved large numbers of people.

The religious wars which raged across France in the 16th century pitting **Protestants** (**Huguenots**) against Catholics also contributed to the decline of the Camino.

In the late 16th century, the Camino received another blow. In 1589, fearing a raid by the English privateer, **Sir Francis Drake,** who had landed at A Coruña, the archbishop of Santiago, **Juan San Clemente**, had the sepulchre containing the relics in the crypt of the cathedral bricked up to keep them safe from the marauding Englishmen.

With the passing of time the exact location of the relics was forgotten, and in reports of major events in the cathedral in the following centuries, no mention is made either of the crypt or the sepulchre. Although, the traditional belief survived that the relics were still to be found underneath the cathedral.

Indeed, the lack of relics never entirely stopped the flow of pilgrims, with the 17th and 18th centuries experiencing a mini-boom, especially in pilgrims from Germany.

REDISCOVERY

In 1879, the then Cardinal of Santiago, **Payá y Rico**, taking advantage of renovation works being carried out on the cathedral, set out to locate the relics. On the night of 28 January they were found behind a wall behind the main altar.

In 1884, **Pope Leo XIII**, after an investigation, the validity of which was severely questioned at the time, issued a Papal Bull, *Omnipotens Deus*, declaring the relics to be those of St James, thus granting Rome's seal of approval.

This revival of the Camino may have had political undertones, coming shortly after the upheavals which culminated in the revolution of 1868, and led to the introduction of limited democracy, freedom of religion and eventually the foundation of a republic in 1873. It also coincided with the rise of Lourdes as Europe's most popular Marian shrine.

The response to this new 'discovery' was noticeably underwhelming, with little growth in the number of pilgrims until the 20th century, when better rail and road connections made pilgrimage to Santiago popular again. However, it was the 1980s before the popularity of walking there began to increase.

The Camino today

The Road to Santiago remained largely abandoned for much of the century following the rediscovery of the relics of St James, in 1879, despite some attempts during Franco's dictatorship to revive it, including making St James the patron of Spain. It reached a statistical nadir in 1978 when the ecclesiastical authorities in Santiago recorded a total of 13 pilgrims arriving on foot in the city.

Despite this, the Camino was never entirely lost, because it lived on in the memories of the people who lived along it, in its architectural heritage, and in the tradition of hospitality of its religious institutions. So, although there were no waymarkings, local people were well aware of its route as it passed through their locality and, then as now, were happy to point pilgrims in the right direction.

Change was in the air however, because in 1965 in Estella, the organisation *Amigos del Camino de Santiago / Friends of the Camino de Santiago*, had been founded. It set itself the practical objective (among others) of making life easier for the small number of pilgrims who walked the route every year, through documentation, waymarking and the provision of accommodation.

In 1985, the UN declared the Camino a World Heritage Site, then in 1987 the Council of Europe declared it a European Cultural Itinerary. When this was followed by a papal visit in 1989, the statistics went ballistic, reaching a modern record of 272,135 pilgrims in the last Holy Year (G), 2010.

The Camino in the future

There are varying opinions about what the future of the Camino holds. Some worry that its popularity will lead to what is special being lost, pointing to Galicia in August, with hordes of pilgrims, some playing music from their mp3 players as they walk, as an example. But there are lots of Caminos (and the alternatives to the Camino Francés are growing in popularity) and outside of July and August, none of the Caminos are overcrowded.

Others think the Camino's current popularity is just a fad and will die down. They may have a point, after several years of strong (Hape Kerkling-driven) growth, the number of German pilgrims has decreased in recent years. However, most other countries grew (between 2011 and 2012: USA by 90%, UK by 57%, Ireland by 44%, Korea by 43%). In the middle ages the peak popularity of the Camino lasted several hundred years, this time around, if you place its revival at 1986, when the numbers arriving in Santiago passed 1,000, we're only in its 3rd decade. What's more, if you ask first-timers if they'll come back, most of them say yes.

The Camino is rapidly becoming a global phenomenon. Confraternities have appeared in many different countries, including some where they never existed before, and are active in providing facilities to pilgrims in their home countries and on the Caminos. Almost every village on the Camino Francés has accommodation of some description, and new pilgrim hostels are opening practically every month, as well as other facilities.

The tourism authorities, especially in Galicia, are pinning great hopes on the Camino to attract more tourists to their region, which has often lost out to better-known regions (with more reliable sunshine). This leads to a certain amount of tension between those who see the Camino in purely spiritual terms, and those who see it as a way of bringing money to some of Spain's poorest regions. On-line forums, especially Spanish ones, often contain disparaging comments about *turigrinos* who use the Camino for a cheap holiday, committing the three deadly sins: taxis, luggage services and hotels (although complaining about the quality of services and over-pricing also seems to count as un-pilgrim-like behaviour). However, since much of the infrastructure of the Camino is independent of any authority, and largely driven by economics, nobody has the ability to impose a test of worthiness to decide who can walk and who can't.

There have been many changes on the Camino since the heady days of 1993, when the numbers arriving in Santiago surpassed 10,000 for the first time in several centuries. Some would say that it has lost something, which is debatable. However, what cannot be denied is that has gained in many ways, and that much of the development has been for the good. Nowadays you can, at least in summer, show up and start walking with no preparation or forethought, picking up the few things you need in the towns and villages along the way, and make it to Santiago with little difficulty.

The Camino has become a great social phenomenon reflecting Western society (and beyond) at the beginning of the 3rd millennium. You can meet almost anybody on the Camino, from young offenders from France accompanied by a (grumpy) social worker to Hollywood celebrities with the paparazzi in tow. Everybody walks it for their own reasons, and most of them expect to get something out of it, and most of them do get something, but often that something isn't what they expected.

Pilgrims in ancient times

WHY DID PEOPLE WALK TO SANTIAGO?

The Canterbury Tales paints a colourful picture of the variety of people and motivations to be found among medieval pilgrims; a knight, a squire, a miller, a bevy of nuns, a clerk, a monk, and various other representatives of all the classes. Their motivations aren't discussed explicitly, but when each is asked to tell a story, their responses range from sermons on the avoidance of idleness to raunchy tales of village life.

The multitudes winding their way to Santiago de Compostela in the Middle Ages appear, from the evidence available to us, to have been equally diverse. Although their motivations varied from the conventionally religious to the profoundly impious, the one main motivating factor seems to have been an easily summarised human emotion (and one which continues to motivate people today) - hope.

Hope moved real multitudes in the late middle ages, up to half a million people left for Santiago each year, by far Europe's largest regular movement of people, and all the more remarkable given that Europe's population at the time was only 70 to 100 millions.

In the Middle Ages, belief in the supernatural was widespread, encouraged by the Church with stories of miracles being attributed to martyrs and saints, especially in proximity to sacred relics. It was a world where many diseases were incurable, and sometimes seen as a punishment. Knowledge of science was almost non-existent and most people received little or no formal education. To people at that time, the prospect of a miracle cure or intervention may have been their only source of hope and well worth the exertion, expense and risk involved in procuring it.

For that reason, among the multitudes travelling the roads of Europe during the long summer days, the sick and the infirm were well represented, as were women and children. All of the social classes were there too, from pennyless beggars to kings and queens.

But hope was not the only motivator. Many travelled for more earthly reasons. Some as a punishment, because, in some places it was a tradition that murderers be made to walk in chains forged from their murder weapon. Some went in search of adventure or just to escape. Others because it was their job to go on pilgrimages on behalf of other people who, for a variety of reasons, wouldn't or couldn't go themselves. Among the living the dead were also represented as many wealthy individuals left monies in their will to fund a pilgrimage to Santiago.

HOW DID THEY TRAVEL?

All but the richest pilgrims travelled on foot and often barefoot. They might, from time to time, have been able to hitch a ride on a farmer's or a trader's cart, or used one of the river ferries which operated when conditions permitted, thus covering relatively long distances quickly, while giving their legs some well-earned rest.

Better-off pilgrims travelled by horse. Medieval horses differed in size, build and breed to modern horses. For travelling long distances, *Palfrey* horses were ideal, because they could move at a four-beat gait, faster than a walk but slower than a canter or gallop, known as an *amble*. The amble was more comfortable for the rider because it was much smoother than a trot or a gallop, especially over uneven surfaces. Palfrey horses could amble at about 12km/h for many hours a day.

The roads they travelled were often no more than tracks suitable for people or horses walking in single-file. The broad, straight, paved roads the Romans built had long since fallen into disrepair. Travelling cross-country was a lot easier then than now because most of the countryside wasn't cordoned off by fences or hedges. The main obstacles were natural ones; rivers and mountains.

Even if they had set off alone, for safety, security and companionship, they tended to fall into informal groups of like-minded individuals with complementary skills, one may have been an experienced pilgrim, another may have known some Latin, another might have been a good hunter or scavenger.

The journey was usually planned to include several pilgrimage sites, which served to break it up into smaller stages and to keep pilgrims' motivation high by offering them intermediate goals, and the possibility of worshipping in several different sites. Pilgrimage sites went to some lengths to be perceived as welcoming to pilgrims, in return, they benefited both economically and in terms of prestige, from pilgrims visiting them. This was in sharp contrast to many other places, where attitudes towards pilgrims ranged from wariness to outright hostility.

Pilgrims from the British Isles and Scandinavia usually travelled to Galicia by ship. In good weather the journey from the south coast of England would have taken about three days. However, the Bay of Biscay is famous for its storms, and the possibility was always present that a ship could be unable to progress due to headwinds or being becalmed. In both of these cases, the situation on-board became critical when the ship ran out of drinking water.

WHEN DID THEY LEAVE? HOW LONG DID THEY TAKE?

The distance travelled each day varied greatly by individual, weather conditions and terrain, but appears to have been largely similar to the distances covered by modern pilgrims - 20km to 40km. This means that the round trip for pilgrims from Central Europe, including rest days and time spent in Santiago, was about six months. If they'd wanted to time their stay to include St James' Day (conveniently moved to mid-summer from its old date under Mozarabic (G) rites, 30 December), they would have needed to leave home around March, an ideal time, just as the snows of winter were clearing from mountain passes and river traffic was resuming as waterways thawed and were swelled by melt-water.

Besides, warmer weather made the necessity of finding accommodation less urgent, and had the additional advantages of being the season when most people were travelling, when wild fruit and nuts were becoming plentiful and when seasonal labour was needed to help with the harvest.

WHAT DID THEY BRING WITH THEM?

The absence of ergonomic backpacks and a more 'relaxed' attitude to personal hygiene, meant that pilgrims tended to travel even more lightly than they do today. The bare minimum was a knife and spoon, a receptacle for water and a little food in a bag carried over the shoulder or hanging off a staff. Money was often carried sown into the hem of clothes or in the soles of shoes. A light fishing net was also useful and a flint for making fire.

Most important, if the pilgrim was well-connected, were letters of introduction which entitled them to free food and accommodation in certain religious institutions. These had the advantage over money of being of little value to thieves.

In the days before Lycra, pilgrims wore the same clothes as other people. However, with time, the Camino dress-code evolved into something resembling an early form of hiking gear, as pilgrims began to wear short overcoats and short leather capes, sometimes with no sleeves, which gave some protection from the elements while not interfering with walking, and could also serve as bedding. A wide-brimmed hat protected against the sun and rain.

Iron-tipped staffs also became popular for their dual function as a weapon and as a walking aid over rough terrain, although, for a time they were illegal in Spain. A dried, hollow pumpkin was used to carry water, or some other beverage, and was usually attached to the top of the staff. What belongings the pilgrim had were carried in an open-topped bag, which was often made of deerskin or cow leather and carried over their shoulder or on their back.

WHERE DID THEY SLEEP?

By the 12th century, the Camino Francés had developed a network of monasteries which, under the Benedictine rules, were duty bound to provide assistance and accommodation to pilgrims. The quality and type of accommodation varied greatly and, at times, the sheer number of pilgrims requiring shelter meant that it was not possible to accommodate everyone.

Monasteries operated on the basis that the services they offered pilgrims should not interfere with or hinder the day-to-day life of the monastery. Pilgrims' quarters were physically separate from the monastery itself and monks and nuns were forbidden from contact with pilgrims without their superior's permission.

The accommodation varied from wooden benches, possibly with straw for bedding, to the luxury of beds with blankets. Sleeping quarters were usually strictly segregated, with men in one area and women and children in another. Food was sometimes provided, but usually for a price, and often pilgrims were expected to provide their own.

Pilgrim hostels (often also called 'hospitals', a name which does not imply any medical function, and shares its Latin root with the English word 'hospitality'), were often located near the summit of mountain passes (such as Somport and Roncesvalles) or at bridges (Hospital de Órbigo), where the flow of pilgrims was funnelled together. They provided basic shelter and warmth, and sometimes a meal. Hostels were founded and run by religious orders or brotherhoods or confraternities of ex-pilgrims, or were sometimes under royal patronage. The simplest hostels consisted of a dormitory and a kitchen. Bigger hostels could include a church, stables, separate dormitories for women and men and a cemetery. Normally, pilgrims were only allowed stay one night.

The main pilgrim routes also developed a network of guest houses, often attached to a tavern where food was served. These establishments had a reputation for disreputable behaviour and were off-limits to the clergy (whether to protect the clergy or other patrons, is not clear). The standards of the accommodation and food varied greatly, and innkeepers' reputation for deviousness was often richly deserved.

Then as now, the knowledge that certain customers were unlikely ever to return, meant that standards in freshness and preparation of food and drink were often lax. Beds often had to be shared with one or more other pilgrims, which on cold nights was considered a bonus. Where no accommodation was available, pilgrims either sought shelter with the local population or, in warm weather, simply made camp in the shelter of a tree.

WHAT DID THEY EAT?

The poorest of pilgrims often depended on their wits and on charity for survival. They scavenged for whatever nuts, berries and fruit were in season. They fished in any river they encountered, and fish provided them with their main source of protein. They knocked on doors of prosperous houses asking for food. In villages and town they stood outside the church, their pilgrim regalia predominately displayed, begging for alms of any description.

The religious orders which were dedicated to offering hospitality to pilgrims were the only reliable refuge for the poorest of the poor. Without them the journey to Santiago would have been impossibly difficult for pilgrims of little or no means.

Coins made of precious metals were the main currency in the Middle Ages. The value of the coin derived from the quantity of metal they contained, rather than any state guarantee. This was largely irrelevant for the poorest in society, who existed in a mostly cashless economy where barter was the main means of exchange. During the harvest, a few hours work was often repaid with a meal and a place to sleep. Begging was mostly rewarded with food or drink, rather than money.

They drank mostly water from village wells, when one was to hand. Otherwise they took their chances with water from streams.

More prosperous pilgrims could supplement their scavenging with food bought in villages and from farms. However, what was available was very dependent on the season, the harvest and the local climate. Meat was expensive, so their diet was largely vegetarian, with some fish. Bread and cheese were widely available year round, as were eggs from chickens or geese. Some kind of ale was often produced locally, and was safer to drink than water from streams. Wine was available but was expensive outside of wine regions.

WHAT RIGHTS / OBLIGATIONS DID PILGRIMS HAVE?

Pilgrims were forbidden from carrying weapons, although their staffs, could be used for self-defence. They were obliged to be of upright and moral behaviour, to refrain from gluttony, drunkenness and licentiousness, to take the sacraments (communion, confession) whenever possible, and generally to practise the Christian virtues, charity, humility, etc., during the course of their pilgrimage. They were also expected to adopt Pilgrim dress, making them easily recognisable to fellow pilgrims and others.

The fact of being a pilgrim also afforded certain rights. Pilgrims were exempt from some tolls, they had the right to avail of free or cheap accommodation and sometimes food, could ask for (and sometimes receive) discounts for river ferries, and were granted the protection of the Church authorities. In some places offences committed against pilgrims attracted especially harsh punishments (including excommunication).

On their return journey they carried a sign to show that they had completed their pilgrimage. For Santiago it was a scallop-shell (G), for Jerusalem a palm leaf from Jericho.

WHAT DIFFICULTIES DID THEY FACE?

One of the principal difficulties for pilgrims was a lack of reliable information. Most pilgrims were illiterate, so their only source of information when planning their journey was from people in their own community who'd walked the route before, or 2nd and 3rd hand accounts, which were often unreliable to the point of being useless. This information could be out-of-date or simply jumbled by the tricks time plays on human memory. Real difficulties could be glossed over or talked down out of bravado or idealism.

The first written guide did not appeared until the 12th century, but even then most pilgrims remained heavily dependant on hearsay.

As a result, it was difficult to gauge accurately the best route to follow and the time, distance and costs involved. Knowledge of geography was vague and imprecise, and pilgrims relied heavily for information on other pilgrims and on local people, who generally had only a limited knowledge of the world beyond their own village.

This was made more difficult by the fact that, within a weeks' walk, and without necessarily having crossed a language boundary, the spoken language of the common people would have changed so much as to make communication difficult. Further along, other languages and dialects added to the difficulty. Since most pilgrims had little or no formal education, their knowledge of other languages was dependant on their having travelled, which most hadn't. Latin was the *lingua franca* from Roman times up until the 18th century, but knowledge of it was mostly confined to the ruling classes and the clergy.

Added to these problems was the lack of standardised units of measure for weight and distance. Coinage too, changed from region to region, and exchange rates fluctuated more or less at random, leaving pilgrims vulnerable to scams by money changers and innkeepers.

There were localised and seasonal food shortages, caused by each region's dependence on local produce, due to the lack of an effective transport infrastructure and reliable methods of preserving food.

Clean drinking water was also sometimes difficult to find, and the Codex Calixtinus goes into quite a lot of detail about which sources of water are safe and which aren't.

WHAT HAZARDS DID THEY FACE?

Freedom from paying tolls and access to pilgrim accommodate meant that there was a strong temptation for unscrupulous individuals to adopt pilgrim dress. These 'pretend pilgrims' were sometimes traders, who combined their visits to customers and suppliers, with a greater or lesser amount of visiting of holy sites, which were numerous enough around Europe to justify almost any journey. Others were less harmless, and it was not unknown for thieves and bandits to disguise themselves as pilgrims in order to appear both trustworthy and inconspicuous.

Genuine pilgrims, who may or may not have been forewarned, had to learn fast to make quick judgements about other pilgrims. Advice about which route to take or which inn to frequent or avoid, had to be carefully weighed to identify attempts to con or to trick, or to lure pilgrims into the wilderness where they could be more easily waylaid.

In the days before centrally controlled nation states, there was little to prevent banditry in open country. In towns and cities the representatives of the reigning sovereign provided law and order and justice, of a type. But once outside the town walls, there was little protection for travellers, and the roads were populated with outlaws ready to rob, and every manner of chancer, charlatan and low-life ready to trick naïve pilgrims out of their money or valuables, sometimes by posing as a holy man or healer. Pilgrims' welfare and sometimes their lives, depended on their judgement of the people they met. In these circumstances it was a good rule to stick close to one's fellow countrymen, and more experienced pilgrims. Apart from the danger to all pilgrims of kidnap, murder and robbery, female pilgrims and children were particularly vulnerable to sexual violence and to being sold into slavery.

Crooked innkeepers also preyed on unsuspecting pilgrims, with tricks such as watering down drinks, and substituting poor wine for good after the first portion had been drunk.

False accusations of theft were also a danger, as the experience of the young German pilgrim in Santo Domingo de la Calzada shows (although, this legend is also associated with Toulouse). Even being accused of a relatively minor theft, such as of a chicken, could lead to the unlucky pilgrim being strung up from the nearest tree. Some religious communities and hostels offered a sanctuary from such mob justice, and the prospect of a fair(er) hearing and more proportionate punishment.

The danger of being kidnapped and held to ransom was another possibility, especially for well-to-do pilgrims. Given the slowness and unreliability of communications, the unfortunate kidnap victim probably would face several months of captivity, in the worst cases, chained hand and foot in a rat-infested dungeon.

Besides banditry and general thuggery, pilgrims also faced dangers from wild animals. Wolves were common in forested areas and wild boars were also common. The high valleys of the Pyrenees were home to populations of bears which were also potentially hazardous to pilgrims, especially those travelling alone.

All of these dangers meant that, as time went on, the military orders of knights - the Knights Templar (G) and Knights of St James (G) - began to play a key role in protecting pilgrims.

ARRIVAL IN SANTIAGO

After months of walking, weary pilgrims eventually arrived in Lavacolla (where Santiago's airport is today), where it was traditional for them to remove their clothing and wash themselves thoroughly before approaching the holy city.

About an hour's walk after Lavacolla, pilgrims arrived on Monte do Gozo / Mount of Joy. From here they got their first sighting of Santiago cathedral in the distance. Although, today this view is somewhat obscured by trees and urban sprawl, in times gone by the cathedral would have towered over other buildings and dominated the landscape.

Arriving at the cathedral the pilgrims, if it was a Holy Year (G), would have entered through *la Puerta Santa / the Holy Door* (G), and taken up position as close as they could get to the sacred relics. If possible, they spent their first night in Santiago in the cathedral itself, singing and praying by candlelight and trying to stay awake. During busy times several hundred pilgrims may have been present in the cathedral overnight, so it is hardly surprising that the ecclesiastical authorities invented the Botafumeiro (G) to try and clear the air in time for mass. Sleeping in churches was later banned outright.

On the following morning at dawn, they presented their offering to the cathedral and confessed their sins. Then, as now, the cathedral sought to ensure that pilgrims were able to confess in their own language by providing priests of different nationalities. Sins confessed, they climbed the steps behind the statue of St James and embraced him from behind: *el abrazo, the embrace.*

From the 14th century onwards, they were presented with a certificate stating that they had completed the pilgrimage in a satisfactory manner.

It's difficult to imagine the awe that a building like the cathedral in Santiago must have struck in the hearts of people who had spent their entire lives in rural communities and had probably never before seen a building with more than two or three storeys.

Pilgrims often stayed for several weeks, revelling in the atmosphere, which was positively festive around St James' Day, and allowing tired legs time to recover from their journey. During this time they might have made the round trip to Finisterre to see the end of the known world and, possibly for the only time in their lives, the sea.

This was also a time of mental and physical preparation for the return journey. Santiago offered a wide range of services to pilgrims, ranging from repair of clothing and footwear to supplies for the journey.

When leaving Santiago, many pilgrims wished to leave something close to the relics in order to maintain a presence there after they themselves had return home. Poor pilgrims would often leave a wooden cross which they had carried from their home, or made themselves en route. Wealthy pilgrims often brought gifts made of precious metals, which then became the property of the cathedral and were usually melted down and minted into coins. Sometimes what was left behind reflected the assistance which had been received or was wished for, such as a crutch or a wooden leg.

Pilgrims would also have taken this opportunity, if they had not already done so, to find a group of pilgrims with whom they shared a language and a route, for the return journey.

HOMECOMING

On the return journey many pilgrims chose to follow a different route to their outward journey. This gave them the opportunity of visiting new holy sites, or of avoiding difficulties encountered on the outward journey.

On arriving home pilgrims were often greeted with spontaneous outpourings of joy and relief from family and friends. Depending on their social status, they may also have merited an ecclesiastical welcoming party and spontaneous ringing of church bells. A returned pilgrim, regardless of their social class, immediately achieved minor celebrity status in their home place and, if they were a good raconteur, probably ate and drank for free for several months.

Given the awe with which returned pilgrims were treated, it would have been surprising if the magnitude of their experience, the trials and tribulations faced, and the miracles and wonders witnessed, had not been exaggerated to some degree in the countless retellings (if only unwittingly).

Pilgrims often kept their pilgrim clothing and other objects, sometimes displaying them prominently in their home, and dusting them off and wearing them for special occasions. Some pilgrims took their shell and their staff to the grave with them.

The images of St James

The image of St James favoured by Church and civil authorities has changed down the centuries. During the **Reconquista** (G) the image most often used was that of **Santiago Matamoros / St James the Moor Slayer**, which seems to originate in the legend of the Battle of Clavijo (G) (where St James, mounted on a white horse, intervened to prevent the defeat of the Christian forces - see page 93).

This image of St James on a white horse with a sword in his hand, killing large numbers of Muslims, was intended to convey a clear message: the Muslims could be defeated and God was on the side of Christianity.

Later, the Reconquista having been brought to a successful end, the image of St James changed to the more familiar one, still commonly used today, that of **Santiago Peregrino / St James the Pilgrim,** dressed in the traditional garb of medieval pilgrims with a prominent scallop-shell on his hat.

In many places both images exist side-by-side, Santiago Cathedral being a prime example. They have in common that they are both examples of a biblical figure re-interpreted (or 're-branded') to suit a different era.

Ethnicities and languages

BASQUES

The Basques inhabit the lands, known as Euskadi or the Basque Country, on both sides of the French / Spanish frontier, where it meets the Atlantic Ocean at the Bay of Biscay. They number today about 3 million, but calculating the exact figure is complicated by the mixing of populations caused by large scale immigration from other parts of Spain into the Spanish Basque Country over the course of the last centuries, to provide workers for the its heavy industries, and by the difficulties associated with trying to fix the frontiers of the Basque Country.

The Basque people are distinguished by their unique culture and language, which has no relation to any other living language. It is the only surviving example of the languages which were spoken in the Iberian peninsula before the Roman conquest. Its survival seems to have been mostly due to a lack of interest on the part of the Romans in conquering the mountainous and isolated Basque Country.

In France, the Basque Country makes up about half of the territory of the department of Pyrénées-Atlantiques. Although Basque identity is strong in the French Basque Country, the desire for independence is weaker than on the Spanish side.

In Spain Basque is officially recognised as a historic nationality (G) by the Constitution.

The Autonomous Region of Navarra is officially bilingual Spanish / Basque. Both languages can be used in the civil administration and Basque is actively promoted in the education system. The Basque-speaking areas are mostly in the mountainous north. Basque speakers make up about 10% of the region's population.

In the Autonomous Region of the Basque Country, use of the language is actively promoted by the regional government and the education system is fully bilingual. As a result a higher percentage of young people speak it than do older people. Native Basque speakers make up about 25% of the population, mostly in the north.

CASTILIANS

The Castile region occupies the whole centre of Spain, taking in the autonomous regions of Castilla y León, Madrid and Castilla la Mancha. Its heartland is the northern *Meseta* (G), from where the Castilian people pushed southwards during the Reconquista (G). The Castilians have been central to Spanish society since then, and continue to play a dominant role in politics, despite the greater prosperity of the Basque Country and Catalonia.

The Spanish language is often referred to as Castellano, or Castilian because it originated in this region. Northern Castile is where the purest form of Spanish is spoken.

The name Castile is believed to have come from the numbers of castles which were built there during the Reconquista and their prominence in the flat landscape of the Mesetas.

CATALANS

Catalan is spoken in the autonomous communities of Catalonia, Valencia and the Balearic Islands, around Perpignon in southern France, in the Principality of Andorra and in a small part of Sardinia. It is a Latin language closely related to the Occitan language of Southern France.

While Catalonia has a strong independence movement the other Catalan-speaking territories seem less inclined to want to break from Spain.

GYPSIES

Iberian Gypsies (*Gitanos*) are a traditionally nomadic people, now mostly settled, distributed across the Iberian peninsula, but mostly in the south. They are related to other Roma groups in Europe, and are believed to have come originally from Northern India.

Spanish Gypsies speak a dialect of Andalusian Spanish called, Caló. They have a strong musical tradition with flamenco singing and dance being its best known manifestations. As with other ethnic minorities in Spain, they were the victims of discrimination and attempted forced assimilation. Today they number about 700,000 people.

Although traditionally Roman Catholic, many Spanish Gypsies and western European Roma have recently converted to Evangelical Protestantism.

LEONESE

The modern Province of León is a smaller version of the Kingdom of León, which dates back to the 10th century and which played a key role in the Reconquista (G).

León was incorporated into the modern Autonomous Community of Castilla y León upon its creation in 1983. Some people argue that an administrative area uniting the traditional regions of León and Castilla la Vieja has no historical precedent and has never been ratified in a popular vote. A movement to separate the two regions exists, as is obvious from the quantity of *León sin Castilla* graffiti which can be seen on the Camino around León.

Although it has its own language (or dialect, depending who you ask), Leonés, it is only spoken in rural areas in the west of the province. It belongs to the linguistic continuum which stretches from the Asturian coast southwards to the province of Zamora and which marks the transition zone between Castilian and Galician.

MARAGATOS

The Maragatos inhabit a region known as the Maragatería which is centred on the village of Santa Colomba de Somoza. The Camino enters the Maragatería through its capital Astorga and leaves it at the boundary of El Bierzo. Whether the Maragatos actually constitute an ethnic group is a matter of some controversy, however, they have a long tradition of distinctive customs and dress, and a reputation for being enterprising and widely travelled.

BERCIANOS

El Bierzo doesn't have a unified regional identity, lying as it does in the transition zone between León and Galicia. The main spoken language is Castilian with some Asturian-Leonese influences, however, in the west (beyond Villafranca) this is replaced by Galician influences.

GALICIANS

Galician is officially recognised as a historic nationality (G) by the Spanish Constitution. Their language is closely related to Portuguese. Although Galicia has pro-independence political movements, the desire among the populace for making the break from Spain doesn't seem to be as strong as in the Basque Country or Catalonia. Despite this, a higher percentage of Galicians speak their language than do Catalans or Basques.

The region was colonised by Celts, as was much of north-western Iberia, around the time of the Roman conquest, but apart from Galician folk music and the ruins of a few round stone buildings, few traces of Celtic culture remain.

The Galician musical instrument which provides the soundtrack in establishments catering to tourists and pilgrims, is the *Gaita*. It is a slightly more subdued version of its Scottish cousin, the bagpipe, and is played in a similar manner with similar lamentable consequences. Its less common relative is the *Gaita de Barquin* which, as with the Irish *uilleann pipes*, is supplied with air from a bellows worked by the player's elbow.

The oldest form of traditional dance in Galicia is called a *muiñeira*. It is danced by groups of men and women in parallel lines or in separate groups to the 'tune' of the *Gaita*.

COMMUNICATING

You don't need to speak any Spanish to walk the Camino Francés. However, you will be dealing with a lot of people who speak only Spanish, knowing a little, can make things a lot easier and more pleasant. The needs of a pilgrim are generally pretty basic, and the communities you'll pass through have been taking care of people like you for centuries, so if you learn a few words for basic stuff (hostel, sleep, shower, wash, plus whatever you like to eat and drink) you'll be fine.

You'll meet many Europeans who speak English as a second language. It's taught more-or-less universally as the main foreign language in European schools, except in some bilingual areas where it comes in third. The variety taught is British English and it's increasingly used as the default *lingua franca*, or bridge language, between people who don't speak each other's languages, replacing French in southern Europe and German and Russian in the east.

Fluency in English has spread like wildfire across the newly democratic countries of Eastern Europe, leaving Southern European countries like Spain struggling to catch up. Eastern Europeans also have fewer hang-ups about speaking English, partially because they see it as the language of freedom and democracy and partially because Eastern Europe is a patchwork of countries and languages and people. So, in their everyday lives, they need a way to communicate with their near neighbours – in a way that the Spanish and French don't.

Also, whereas until recently French to some extent rivalled English as Europe's *lingua franca*, this is no longer the case.

So, if a Finn and an Italian (or a Latvian and a Lithuanian) meet on the Camino, they'll probably speak English together. In the new Europe, where people travel much more for work and leisure, speaking English with other non-native speakers is becoming increasingly common, which has led to the development of a variety of English based on *English as a Foreign Language* (EFL), as taught in schools, with a smaller vocabulary and simplified grammar, mixed together with a lot of influences from television, films, popular music, the internet and video games.

You would think that this would make life easy for native English speakers, but, ironically EFL speakers often understand other EFL speakers a lot better than they do native speakers, simply because we talk too fast and too idiomatically and, since we're not all from Oxford or Cambridge, we have every manner of strange accent. International conferences often tick along swimmingly in English, until the American or (heaven help us all) the Scot, stands up to speak, leaving delegates understanding 50% or 10% respectively.

So, if you're a native English speaker and nobody (except the Dutch and the Scandinavians) understands you, try the following:

- Speak slowly (not ridiculously slowly, just more slowly than you usually do)
- Use simple, short sentences (again, not ridiculously...)
- Avoid idioms and 'overpoliteness'

An **idiom** is an expression whose meaning isn't clear just from the meaning of the words. eg. *He has a chip on his shoulder.* These are expressions which will receive blank looks and end up with you having to explain.

An example of **overpoliteness** would be *Do you think I could have some ice in my drink?* Because this is phrased like you're asking somebody's opinion, it is guaranteed to confuse. All you have to say is *Ice* and point.

Finally. English is a commonly spoken language in Europe but it is not a neutral language, in that it belongs to a specific culture (*Anglo-American,* also often misleadingly called *Anglo-Saxon*). It is also imposed, in that most Europeans now are obliged to learn English in school. They don't get a choice. So, when people speak English with you, remember that they're doing you a favour. A small effort with other peoples' language (even if it's just the word for *hello*) shows that you recognise and respect their culture, and goes a small way towards redressing the linguistic imbalance. Your small effort will probably be repaid many times over in trust and friendship.

Spanish language guide

The Spanish generally appreciate any effort foreigners make to speak their language, even if you do it badly. This language guide is not an attempt to impart on you a subtle understanding of the language. The aim is to give you a few words and phrases you might find useful on the Camino, so that hopefully you won't have to resort to animal noises and chicken imitations.

Spanish people use the (informal) *tú* form for *you,* as opposed to the (formal) *Usted,* with reckless abandon. This can be quite hair-raising if you learned French and had it drummed into you to always use the polite form unless invited to do otherwise. No disrespect is intended in addressing you as *tú*. It's just a symptom of the tendency towards informality and egalitarianism in modern Spain.

Spanish is pronounced (to a very large degree) as it's written. The best way to learn Spanish pronunciation is from listening to examples. For links to some good Spanish-for-beginners websites see:

www.lingolex.com/pronounce or *www.studyspanish.com/pronunciation*

The BBC also has some good resources for getting a grip of the basics of the language: *www.bbc.co.uk/languages/spanish*

GENDERS

Spanish, like other Latin languages, has masculine and feminine versions of nouns and adjectives. Masculine versions usually (but not always) end in -*o* and feminine in -*a*. eg. **una chica = a girl, un chico = a boy**

Plurals of nouns and adjectives are formed by adding -*es* if the word ends in a consonant and -*s* if it ends in a vowel: *casa / casas, autobús / autobuses*

NUMBERS

0 Cero	1 Uno / Una	2 Dos
3 Tres	4 Cuatro	5 Cinco
6 Seis	7 Siete	8 Ocho
9 Nueve	10 Diez	11 Once
12 Doce		

TELLING THE TIME

When written down, times are usually written in 24-hour format. In informal speech the 12-hour format is usually used with *de la mañana* = a.m. and *de la tarde* = p.m.

La una = One o'clock
Las dos = Two o'clock
Las seis de la mañana = 06:00 / 6 a.m.
Las diez de la tarde = 22:00 / 10 p.m.
Las dos y media = Half past two
La mañana = Morning (por la mañana = in the morning)
La tarde = Evening or afternoon (por la tarde = in the evening)
Hoy = Today
Ayer = Yesterday
Mañana = Tomorrow
Más tarde = Later
Pronto = Early
Tarde = Late
En seguida = Soon

MENU GUIDE

COOKING TECHNIQUES

A la Brasa = Grilled
Asado = Roasted
Frito = Fried
Guisado = Stewed
Hervido = Boiled

PRIMERO OR ENTREMESES / STARTER

Ensalada Verde = Green Salad (lettuce, tomatoes, tuna)
Ensaladilla Rusa = Russian Salad (potatoes, peas, tuna, mayonnaise)
Judías Verdes = Green Beans
Macarrones = Pasta, usually with some kind of sauce. Spanish pasta, or *macarrones*, as it's usually called, is really the poor relative of its Italian cousin. It may start out the same, but after it's been cooked for half an hour and mixed with some grotesque supermarket heat-and-eat sauce, this most simple of staples has become something you would hesitate to give to your worst enemy.
Sardinas = Sardines
Sopa = Soup (de verduras / vegetables, pollo / chicken, lentejas / lentils, etc.)

SEGUNDO OR PLATO PRINCIPAL / MAIN COURSE

Albóndigas = Meatballs
Atún = Tuna

Chorizo = Cured smoked sausage
Chuleta de Cerdo = Pork Chop
Cocido = Stew
Cordero = Lamb
Costilla = Pork Cutlet
Croquetas = Fried rolled potato, sometimes with a meat or fish filling
Embuchados = Lamb intestines
Hígado = Liver
Huevo = Egg
Jamón = Ham
Jamón Serrano = Cured Ham
Lacón = Shoulder of Pork
Paella = Rice with seafood and/or chicken
Patatas = Potatoes
Patatas Bravas = Fried potatoes with a 'spicy' sauce
Patatas Fritas = Chips (or French Fries)
Pescado (del Día) = Fish (of the Day)
Pollo = Chicken
Pulpo (en su tinta) = Octopus (in its ink)
Pulpo a la Gallega / Pulpo Galego = Boiled Galician Octopus
Salchicha = Sausage
Solomillo = Sirloin
Ternera = Beef

COOKING MEAT
Poco hecho = Rare
Al punto = Medium
Muy hecho = Well done

POSTRE / DESSERT
Arroz con Leche = Rice Pudding
Cuajada = Creamy substance often served with honey
Flan = Crème Caramel
Fruta = Fruit
Helado = Ice Cream
Mousse = Mousse
Natillas = Custard
Pudding = Sweet, gooy substance, no English equivalent
Torta de Santiago = Tart made with almonds (almendras)
Tarta = Tart, comes in various flavours

MISCELLANEOUS FOOD
Aceite de Oliva = Olive Oil
Agua = Water
Carne = Meat
Comedor = Dining room
Cocina = Kitchen
Gaseosa = Soft drink/Mineral/Soda

Pan = Bread
Sal = Salt
Seta = Wild mushroom
Vinagre = Vinegar

VEGETABLES / VERDURAS
Ajo = Garlic
Berenjena = Aubergine
Cebolla = Onion
Lechuga = Lettuce
Tomate = Tomato
Zanahoria = Carrot

UTENSILS
Cuchara = Spoon
Cuchillo = Knife
Tenedor = Fork

MEALS
Almuerzo = Lunch (almorzar = to eat lunch)
Cena = Dinner (cenar = to eat dinner)
Desayuno = Breakfast (desayunar = to eat breakfast)

DESAYUNO / BREAKFAST
Café con Leche = Coffee with steamed milk
Colacao = Hot chocolate made from milk
Zumo de Naranja = Orange Juice
Croissant = Croissant
Desayuno = Breakfast, usually fairly Spartan
Magdalena = Sweet Bun (like a small muffin)
Napolitana = Chocolate Danish/Pain au Chocolat
Pan con Aceite = Toast with Olive Oil
Pan con Tomate = Toast with ground tomato. You may have to do the grinding
  yourself.
Tostadas = Toast normally served with butter (*mantequilla*) and jam (*mermelada*)

SNACKS / PARA PICAR
Aceitunas = Olives
Bocadillo (also occasionally Bocata) = Sandwich, usually served in an enormous
  bread roll
Cacahuete = Peanut
Chocolate = Chocolate
Empanada = Pie with tuna, meat or vegetables filling
Frutos secos = Nuts
Patatas fritas = Crisps (potato chips)
Queso = Cheese
Raciones = Like tapas but bigger
Tortilla = Spanish Omelette
Tortilla de Patata = Spanish Omelette with potato

Tortilla Española = Omelette with ham and onion
Tortilla Francesa = French Omelette

FRUIT / FRUTA

Fruta = Fruit
Manzana = Apple
Naranja = Orange
Paraguayo = Flat peaches
Plátano = Banana
Uvas = Grapes

TAPAS / PINCHOS

Tapas are snacks served in cafés, usually displayed on the counter. **Pinchos** is the Basque for Tapas (sometimes also written **Pinxos**). Common Tapas are:

Aceitunas = Olives
Albóndigas = Meatballs
Boquerones = Anchovies
Calamares or Rabas = Rings of fried Squid
Chorizo al Vino = Sausage cooked in Wine
Croquetas = Croquettes
Empanadas or Empanadillas = Pie with Meat, Fish or Vegetables
Ensaladilla Rusa = Russian Salad
Gambas = Prawns
Patatas Bravas = Fried Diced Potatoes with a 'spicy' sauce
Tortillas = Omelettes.

DRINKS ETC. / BEBIDAS ETC.

HOT DRINKS

Azúcar = Sugar
Café (or Café Solo) = Espresso
Café con Leche = Coffee with Steamed Milk
Café Cortado = Espresso with a dash of milk
Colacao = Hot chocolate
Taza = Cup
Té = Tea (although Spain is NOT a tea-drinking nation)

ALCOHOLIC DRINKS

Cerveza = Beer (more commonly in cafés you would ask for *una caña* which means a draft beer). Sometimes they haven't got draught in which case you'll get *una botella* – a bottle (33cl), or *un botellín* – a small bottle (20cl).
Cerveza sin alcohol = Alcohol-free beer
Clara de Limón = Beer with lemonade (Shandy)
Hielo = Ice
Sidra = Apple cider
Tinto de Verano = Red wine, lemonade, lemon, ice
Vaso or Copa = Glass
Vino = Wine
Vino Blanco = White Wine

Vino Rosado = Rosé
Vino Tinto = Red Wine (literally *coloured wine*)

NON-ALCOHOLIC DRINKS

Many international soft drinks, such as Coca Cola, Fanta, are commonly available.
Agua con gaz = Sparkling water
Agua del grifo = Tap water
Agua natural = Still water (this is the norm)
Gaseosa = Soft drink
Zumo de naranja = Orange juice

ACCOMMODATION

Although the Spanish word *albergue* is the most common word for hostel, on the Camino you will occasionally see the word *refugio*. These two words have the same meaning in the context of the Camino.

Donativo or *La Voluntad* are used to describe a hostel which asks for a donation rather than a fixed payment. These hostels continue to exist thanks to the generosity of pilgrims. The word for free is gratuito or gratis.

The word *hostal* means a family-run guest-house, often with shared bathrooms, *habitaciones* means rooms for rent, *casa rural, hospedaje, pensión*, all mean some form of guest house, *parador* means a posh hotel in a historic building, and *hotel* has basically the same meaning as in English.

Cama = Bed
Albergue de peregrinos = Pilgrim hostel (occasionally *refugio*)
Almohada = Pillow
Baño = Bathroom (¿Dónde esta el baño? = where is the bathroom?)
Cocina = Kitchen (Cocino, cocinamos = I, we cook)
Colchón = Mattress
Ducha = Shower (Me ducho = I'm having a shower)
Habitación = Room (in hotel, etc.)
Hospitalera/Hospitalero = hostel warden
Lavar = To wash (lavar ropa = wash clothes)
Llave = Key (La llave del albergue = the key of the hostel)
Saco de dormir = Sleeping bag

DIRECTIONS

¿Cuántos kilómetros? = How many kilometres?
¿Dónde esta...? = Where is...? (¿Dónde esta la tienda? = Where is the shop?)
Carretera = Road (¡Vamos por la carretera! = Lets walk on the road!)
Cerca = Near (La tienda esta cerca de la iglesia = The shop is near the church)
Ciudad = City
Derecha = Right (a la derecha = to the right)
Detrás = Behind (El albergue esta detrás de la iglesia = the hostel is behind the church)
En = In
En Frente = Opposite
Flecha (Amarilla) = (Yellow) Arrow
Iglesia = Church

Izquierda = Left (a la izquierda = to the left)
Lejos = Far (No esta tan lejos = It's not that far)
Pueblo = Village/Town
Puente = Bridge
Río = River
Todo recto = straight ahead (sometimes just *recto*)

FACILITIES

Agua No Potable = Water not fit for human consumption
Agua Potable = Drinking Water
Autobús = Bus (El autobús por Madrid = The bus to Madrid)
Cerrado = Closed (La iglesia esta cerrada = The church is closed)
Farmacia = Chemist / Pharmacist
Frutería = Vegetable/Fruit Shop
Fuente = Drinking Fountain
Panadería = Bakery
Pastelería = Cake shop
Periódicos = Newsagents
Piscina = Swimming pool
Supermercado = Supermarket
Tabacos = Cigarettes shop
Tienda = Grocery Shop, also sells alcohol (you'll also see them called *Comestibles* and *Alimentación*)

HEALTH

Alergia = Allergy
Ampolla = Blister
Centro de Salud = Health Centre
Dolor = Pain
Hospital = Hospital
Médico = Doctor
Rodilla = Knee
Pierna = Leg
Pié = Foot

WEATHER

Cubierto = Overcast
Chubascos = Showers
Despejado = Clear skys
Frío = Cold
Heladas = Frost
Hoy = Today
Lluvia = Rain
Mañana = Tomorrow
Niebla = Fog
Nieve = Snow
Nubes = Clouds
Tormenta = Storm

Variable = Changeable
Viento = Wind

DAYS OF THE WEEK

Lunes = Monday
Martes = Tuesday
Miércoles = Wednesday
Jueves = Thursday
Viernes = Friday
Sábado = Saturday
Domingo = Sunday

TRAVEL

Aeropuerto = Airport
Autobús = Bus
Bicicleta (or *Bici*) = Bicycle
Billete = Ticket (airplane, train, bus, etc.)
Estación de Autobuses = Bus Station
Estación de Trenes = Railway Station
Horario = Timetable
Ida y Vuelta = Return (as in ticket)
Parada de Autobuses = Bus Stop
Sólo Ida = One way (as in ticket)
Taxi = Taxi

MONEY

Banco = Bank (*La banca* means the banking industry)
Barato = Cheap (also *económico*)
Cajero Automático = Cash Machine (ATM)
Cambio = Bureau de Change / Exchange Office
Caro = Expensive
Céntimos = Eurocents
Dinero = Money
Euros = Euros

USEFUL VERBS

Verbs are the most difficult part of Spanish and the following is intended to give you a few forms which may come in useful rather than teach you how the verb system works.

Ser = to be (permanent states): Soy irlandés (or irlandesa) I'm Irish
Estar = to be (temporary states): Estoy cansado (or cansada) I'm tired
Comer = to Eat
Beber = to Drink
Hablar = to Talk/Speak
Pagar = to Pay
Coger = to Get/Take (does not have the same meaning as in Latin America)
Curar = to Heal

GREETINGS AND WELL WISHES

Hola = Hello, informal but very commonly used
Buen Camino = only used on the Camino, it means something like, *have a good Camino*
Buenos días = Good Morning/Day
Buenas tardes = Good Evening
Buenas noches = Good Night
¿Qué tal? = How are you?
¡Bien! = Well! In reply to, ¿Qué tal?
Buen Provecho = Bon Appétit / Enjoy your meal
Adiós = Bye
Hasta luego = See you later

WEIGHTS AND MEASURES

Kilómetro = Kilometre (km)
Metro = Metre (m)
Gramo = Gramme (g)
Kilogramo (or Kilo) = Kilogramme (kg)

MISC

Sí = Yes
No = No
Gracias = Thanks
Por favor = Please
Perdón = Excuse me/Sorry
De nada = It's nothing/Don't mention it
Servicios/Aseos = Toilets (in cafés, restaurants)
Papel higiénico = Toilet paper (en los servicios no hay papel higiénico = there's no toilet paper in the bathroom)
Credencial = Pilgrim Passport
Sello = Stamp (for letters and Credencial)
Vale = OK
Buen/Bueno/Buena = Good
Mal/Malo/Mala = Bad
Nada = Nothing
Aquí = Here
Allí = There
Grande = Big
Pequeño = Small
Bota = Boot
Zapatos = Shoes
Más = More
Menos = Less
Palo = Stick/Staff
Mochila = Backpack
Botella = Bottle
Meseta = The Plains

Montaña = Mountain
Barro = Mud
Entrada = Entrance / Entry
Salida = Exit / Way Out
Más = More
Menos = Less / Fewer
Mucho (m) / Mucha (f) = a lot, eg. muchos kilómetros
Sobre = On
Arriba = Above
Debajo = Below
Chica = girl / Chico = boy
Se Abre a las... = We open at...
Oficina de Correos = Post Office
Lista de correos = Poste Restante / General Delivery
Zurrón = Goatskin bag

NATIONALITIES

Masculine and feminine forms are given:
Alemán / Alemana = German (Alemania)
Australiano / Australiana = Australian (Australia)
Belga / Belga = Belgian (Bélgica)
Canadiense / Canadiensa = Canadian (Canadá)
Checo / Checa = Czech (la República Checa)
Croata / Croata = Croatia (Croacia)
Eslovaco / Eslovaca = Slovak (Eslovaquia)
Escocés / Escocesa = Scottish (Escocia)
Español / Española = Spanish (España)
Estadounidense / Estadounidensa = USA (los Estados Unidos / EE.UU.)
Finlandés / Finlandesa = Finnish (Finlandia)
Francés / Francesa = French (Francia)
Galés / Galesa = Welsh (Gales)
Holandés / Holandesa = Dutch (Países Bajos)
Inglés / Inglesa = English (Inglaterra)
Irlandés / Irlandesa = Irish (Irlanda)
Italiano / Italiana = Italian (Italia)
Neozelandés / Neozelandesa = Kiwi (Nueva Zelanda)
Polaco / Polaca = Polish (Polonia)
Sueco / Sueca = Swedish (Suecia)
Suizo / Suiza = Swiss (Suiza)

INFORMATION AND WARNING SIGNS

Agua sin garantías sanitarias = Water not guaranteed suitable for consumption
Atención = Attention
Cerrado = Closed
Coto privado de caza = Private hunting
Cruce = Crossing, for a busy road
No apta para consumo = Not suitable for consumption (water)
Peligro = Danger

Playa fluvial = River beach (for swimming)
Privado = Private
Prohibido descalzarse = It is forbidden to remove your shoes
Prohibido fumar = No smoking
Prohibido la entrada = No entry
Se Vende = For sale
WC exclusivo clientes = Toilets/restrooms for customers only

USEFUL PHRASES

Abierto = Open (¿A qué hora abra la tienda? = What time does the shop open?)
No hablo español = I don't speak Spanish
No entiendo = I don't understand
¡La Cuenta! = The bill (check) in a restaurant
¿Cuándo? = When?
¿Qué? = What?
¿Donde esta...? = Where is...? ¿Donde esta el albergue de peregrinos? = Where is the pilgrim hostel?
¿Por qué? = Why?
¡Qué calor! = It's hot (bizarrely, Spanish people begin to complain about the heat as soon as the temperature goes above 20°C)
¡Qué frío! = It's cold (ie. Under 20°C)
La llave del Albergue = the key of the hostel
¿Esta abierto hoy el albergue? = Is the hostel open today?
Hay... = there is... Very useful word. Any of the following Spanish phrases can be a question or a statement.
    ¿Hay pan? = Do you sell bread?
    ¿Hay bocadillos? = Do you sell sandwiches?
    ¿Hay una tienda en el pueblo? = Is there a shop in the village?
No hay... = there isn't... No hay pan = There's no bread
Cuánto? = How much/many?
Cuánto cuesta? = How much does it cost?
Soy vegetariano/vegetariana = I'm a vegetarian.
Sin = Without; sin carne = without meat; sin atún = without tuna

Names for the Camino

The Camino de Santiago is known in English as **The Way of St James** or **St James' Way**. However, English speakers on the Camino almost always refer to it by its Spanish name, **Camino de Santiago**, or just **The Camino**.

The use of the term the Camino can be confusing because, really, there is more than one Camino. Strictly speaking, the Camino from Saint-Jean to Santiago is called the **Camino Francés** / the **French Way**. But, because this is the main and best known Camino, it is often referred to as *the Camino*.

In Spanish it is usually called **El Camino** or **El Camino de Santiago**.

In French it is called **Le Chemin de St Jacques** or just **Le Chemin**. Jacques is the French for James.

In German it is called **der Jakobsweg**. German speaking pilgrims also sometimes use the word **Sternenweg** meaning the way of the stars. Jakob is the German for James.

In Basque it is known as **Donejakue Bidea**.

In Galician, **O Camiño de Santiago** or just **O Camiño**. However you will also see **Ruta Xacobea**.

Galician language guide

The Galician language, *Galego*, is a Latin language closely related to Portuguese, from which it began to diverge after the establishment of an independent Portuguese kingdom in 1139. Approximately 91% of Galician residents claim to speak Galician, making it the strongest of Spain's regional languages.

The language is most commonly spoken in rural areas where it is the community language. Unfortunately, these are also the areas which are experiencing loss of population in favour of the cities due to lack of economic opportunities, and which, as a consequence have an older age profile. Although usage is fairly evenly distributed across age groups, this data may be distorted by education policies which prioritise the teaching of Galician in schools.

All the major cities are mainly Spanish speaking and it seems clear that the future of the Galician language will be decided there.

There are two Galician orthographies. The one used officially is heavily influenced by Spanish. You're unlikely to come across the other except where the word for Galicia is sometimes spelled Galiza.

SOME GALICIAN PHRASES

Ola = Hello
Bo Día = Good Morning/Day
Grazas = Thank you
Adeus = Bye
Por Favor = Please
Galego = Galician (Spanish Gallego)

GALICIAN FOR SPANISH SPEAKERS

If you know some Spanish, it's fairly easy to understand written Galician, at least on a basic level. The most obvious differences between Spanish and Galician include:
The way Galician drops certain consonants and replaces them with a diphthong:

English	Spanish	Galician
Health	Salud	Saude
Middle	Media	Meia

The way certain consonants replace others (*r* replaces *l*)

English	Spanish	Galician
White	Blanco	Branco
Square	Plaza	Praza

x replaces *j*, as in the ubiquitous:

Government of Galicia / Junta de Galicia / Xunta de Galicia

English	Spanish	Galician
To help	Ajudar	Axudar

However, unlike Spanish *j*, *x* is pronounced similar to an English *ch* as in *church*.
Vowel changes: *e* becomes *ei*, and, *ue* becomes *o*

English	Spanish	Galician
Ferry	Crucero	Cruceiro
Port	Puerta	Porta

Galician, like Portugeses, contracts commonly used word combinations into one:

English	Spanish		Galician	
in the	en la	na	(feminine)
in the	en el	no	(masculine)
from/of the	de la	da	(feminine)
from/of the	del	do	(masculine)

The words for *the*

English	Spanish	Galician	
The	La	A	(feminine)
The	El	O	(masculine)

The plurals are *as* and *os*.

Basque language guide

The Basque language is called *Euskadi*. It is a **language isolate,** in that it is unrelated to any other living language, although it has borrowed many words from Latin and Spanish.

Basques are very proud of their language and will be surprised and delighted if you know and use any expressions in it. (However, a word of caution; the policy of promoting regional languages is not without its opponents.)

SOME EUSKADI PHRASES

Egunon / Kaixo= Hello	Arratsaldeon = Good Evening
Zer moduz? = How are you?	Agur = Bye
Ondo ibili = Buen Camino	Eskerrik asko = Thank you
Kontuz! = Attention! (on roadsigns)	

APPENDIX

Glossary

Abertzale (Basque, roughly translates as patriot) used in Spanish to describe the radical left-wing sections of Basque nationalism.

Auto-da-fé (Portuguese act of faith; also auto-de-fe) the ritual of public penance of condemned heretics and apostates that took place when the Inquisition had decided their punishment (that is, after the trial).

Alfonso VI (el Bravo / the Brave) (1047-1109) was king of the Kingdom of León and later of Galicia and Castile, having first defeated his younger brother García of Galicia and later his elder brother Sancho II (el fuerte) of Castile. By taking and holding Toledo he became the first Christian ruler to achieve significant territorial advances against Al-Andalus. These advances were mostly reversed by Muslim counter-attacks led by Berbers from a strict Muslim sect, the Almorávide, newly arrived from north Africa. He is buried in Sahagún.

Al-Mansur (938-1002, full name, Abu 'Amir Muhammad ben Abi 'Amir al-Ma'afirí, known in Spanish as Almanzor) born of noble birth in the vicinity of Algeciras he rose through the ranks of Muslim nobility to become unrivalled leader of Al-Andalus in 981 thus beginning one of the short periods during which Al-Andalus was united under a single ruler. His unrivalled position of power allowed him to concentrate on harrying the Christian states of northern Spain, waging war mostly against León and Castile, he also found time to sack Barcelona (985), Sahagún (988), Santiago de Compostela (997), Pamplona (999) and San Millán de la Cogolla (1002).

Año Santo Jacobeo (Holy Year of St James) when St James' Day (25 July) falls on a Sunday, because the relics of St James are said to have been found on a Sunday. It was instigated by Pope Calixtus II (G). During a Holy Year pilgrims arriving in Santiago by any means who pray in the cathedral and receive the sacraments of communion and confession within 15 days of their visit are granted a plenary indulgence. Pilgrims arriving in any other year receive an indulgence.

Apse (Spanish Ábside) of churches, is the semi-circular recess with a vaulted or domed roof, usually at the eastern end of the building where the altar is. Typical of the Romanesque and Gothic styles.

Archivolt (Spanish Arquivolta) is an ornamental molding or band following the curve of the underside of an arch. See en.wikipedia.org/wiki/Archivolt

Ayuntamiento townhall

Barbican a fortified gateway or any other tower over a gate or bridge, principally on the outer defences of a town or castle.

Blind Arch a decorative arch on a wall which has no opening. Popular on Romanesque and Gothic buildings.

Botafumeiro the gigantic incense burner which hangs from the centre of Santiago cathedral and is swung, while lit, above the heads of the congregation. Besides its ceremonial role it is rumoured to have served the purpose of masking the smell of the masses of pilgrims assembled below.

Bourbon, House of is an important royal house which originated in Navarra in the 16th century. At different times it ruled France, Spain and parts of Italy. Spain (King Juan Carlos) and the Grand Duchy of Luxembourg (Grand Duke Henri) currently have Bourbon monarchs.

Calixtus II, Pope from 1119 until his death in 1124. Born Guy de Vienne to a family of French nobles. Played an important role in establishing Santiago as a pilgrimage site by giving it the right to grant indulgences and establishing the tradition of Holy Years. He also provided funding for the reconstruction of the cathedral after its destruction by Al-Mansur (G).

Capital (architecture) head or cornice of pillar or column.

Charlemagne (742-814, from Latin Carolus Magnus, Charles the Great. Spanish Carlomagno or simply Carlos) was king of the Franks (G) from 768 until his death in 814. He extended the Frankish Kingdoms into an Empire that united much of Western and Central Europe under a single leader for the first time since the fall of Rome. He is associated with the Carolingian Renaissance, a flourishing of art, religious thought and culture. Legend tells that St James appeared to Charlemagne urging him to liberate his tomb in Galicia from Muslim rule.

Cid or El Cid (circa 1041-1099, from colloquial Arabic sidi meaning lord) Born in Vivar near Burgos. Served as a soldier under various Christian kings rising through the ranks until, following a falling-out with King Alfonso VI, he went into exile. He next fought as a mercenary for the Muslim ruler of Zaragoza, al-Mutamin, against his brother with whom he was locked in bitter rivalry. Later he succeeded in capturing and holding a large region around the city of Valencia which he ruled independently despite being theoretically subservient to King Alfonso. He ruled over an ethnically mixed population in this region until his death. His body lies, together with that of his wife Jimena, in Burgos cathedral.

Clavijo, Battle of legendary battle, reputed to have taken place in 844, between Christian and Muslim forces near Logroño, at which St James, mounted on a white horse, assisted the Christian forces. It is usually taken as the origin of the legend of Santiago Matamoros/St James the Moorslayer.

Cluny, Monastery of in Bourgogne in eastern France, founded in 910 by the Benedictine order. It inspired a series of reforms in monastic life aimed at reducing corruption. The monastery was answerable directly to the Pope rather than to any local authorities and had a policy of strict control over its subservient monasteries. The Cluny reforms spread to Spain along the Camino Francés, changing monastic life and replacing the old Mozarabic (G) rites. Much of the monastery was destroyed during the French Revolution, although it has been subsequently been rebuilt.

Codex Calixtinus (Latin Calixtinus Code, aka Liber Sancti Iacobi) written in Latin in the 12th century, it is widely regarded as being the first guide to the Camino de Santiago. In reality the guide is only one of five books and two appendices covering (in order): **I.** Liturgical Anthology, the largest section being almost half the entire manuscript, with detailed instructions about ceremonies and masses. **II.** Book of Miracles, lists the 22 miracles attributed to St James. **III.** Journey of St James' body to Santiago, covers the evangelisation of Spain by St James, his body's journey to Santiago and the custom of the early pilgrims to collect a shell from the Galician coast. **IV.** Conquest of Charlemagne, recounts how St James appeared to Charlemagne in a dream to ask him to liberate his tomb from the Muslims, the battle of Roncesvalles and the death of Roland. **V.** Pilgrims Guide, is a detailed description of the routes to Santiago divided into stages with information about accommodation, drinking water, holy sites, populations, etc. It also contains an extremely in depth guide to the cathedral in Santiago. **Appendix I**, Pontifical Works, including sacred music to be used in the rites. **Appendix II**, is believed to have been added later and makes historical claims which are disputed by modern historians. The Codex was probably written by a number of different authors and then compiled into a single volume by Aymeric Picaud, a French monk, around 1135. The oldest known copy, dating from around 1150, was held in the archives of Santiago Cathedral. This was discovered in 1886 having been lost for several centuries. It the summer of 2011 it was stolen and was missing for over a year until it was found in the home of an employee of the cathedral

Conquistador (Spanish for conqueror) is the word generally used for the people who conquered large parts of the Americas for Spain.

Counter-Reformation a movement within the Catholic Church, beginning with the Council of Trent (circa 1563), which sought to counter the claims and criticisms made by the Reformation.

Five Good Emperors of Rome, are Nerva, Trajan, Hadrian, Antoninus Pius and Marcus Aurelius. They ruled between 96 and 161. Their rule oversaw a period of expansion and consolidation of Roman territory, reform in government and the Romanisation of the various subject peoples.

Franks (also *Frankish*, Spanish *franco*) a group of tribes from western Germany who gradually extended their influence westwards into Gaul (G), founding there the Frankish empire which lasted for several centuries up until the 8th century. In placenames it can also refer to tradesmen and traders who were free of vassalage to noblemen or the Church. Although, is Spain it was often used just to refer to the French.

Gaita a type of bagpipe, which exists in several regions of Spain, being particularly synonymous with Galicia.

Gaul the Roman province covering much of modern-day France.

Gaudí (1852-1926, full name Antoni Gaudí i Cornet) was a Spanish/Catalan architect of the Modernist movement. Among his most famous works are the Sagrada Família cathedral and Park Güell in Barcelona. On the Camino Francés he designed the Episcopal Palace in Astorga.

Hapsburg, House of is an important royal house which originated in Switzerland and over a period of six centuries provided many of the rulers of Austria, the Holy Roman Empire, Spain (and parts of its empire), Burgundy, Bohemia and Hungary.

Historic Nationality under Spain's 1978 constitution three historic nationalities are defined: Catalan, Basque and Galician. Their regions have a constitutional right to self-government within a unified Spanish nation.

Holy Door (Spanish La Puerta Santa) giving entry to the cathedral from Praza da Quintana is opened only during a Holy Year (G).

Holy Year see Año Santo Jacobeo

Hospital is an old word for hostel. It is still in use today in the English 'hospitality' and Spanish 'hospitalero'.

Hospitalero/Hospitalera m/f (Spanish) a person who runs a pilgrim hostel.

Indulgence in Roman Catholic theology, is the full or partial remission of punishment due for sins which had previously been forgiven in the sacrament of Confession.

Jet is a mineraloid derived from decaying wood which has been subjected to prolonged pressure. It is dark in colour and is sometimes used in jewellery.

Knights Hospitaller a religious military order founded in Jerusalem in the 11th century to provide care and assistance for pilgrims to the Holy Lands.

Knights of St James (or Knights of Santiago) a religious military order founded in Spain in the 12th century. The order grew rapidly in power and wealth, accumulating property in Spain and other countries. Besides providing assistance and protection to pilgrims, they participated militarily in the Reconquista (G).

Knights Templar a religious military order closely associated with the Crusades and originally established to provide protection to pilgrims travelling to Jerusalem. They were officially endorsed by the Church around 1129 and grew rapidly in membership and power. They were distinguishable by their white robes with a red cross. Besides fighting in the Crusades, they undertook infrastructural development and law enforcement, especially in relation to pilgrimages. They were disbanded in 1312, having fallen out of favour with the French king, who was financially indebted to them.

Meseta (Spanish for plateau) the flat, central part of the Camino Francés.

Modillion (Spanish modillón) is a support or bracket, whether ornamental or real, for an overhanging part of a building (cornice).

Moor (Spanish moro/mora) is a historical term for the Muslims from North Africa who colonised southern Spain. Although the term implies that the Muslims who arrived in Spain came from one ethnic group, in reality they were a cross-section of North African society where (then as now) the indigenous Berbers (aka Amazighs) lived side-by-side with Arab colonists.

Morisco/Morisca m/f (Spanish for little Moor) a person of Muslim origin who had converted to Christianity, often under coercion.

Mudéjar (Arabic mudajjan meaning permitted to remain) the Muslims who remained in Spain after the Reconquista.

Opus Dei (Latin God's Work) a Roman Catholic organisation sometimes accused of being elitist and of having a secret membership drawn from the rich and powerful. Encourages its members to inflict pain on themselves. The following quotes are from its website www.opusdei.org 'Opus Dei does not publish members' names but leaves it to them to tell people themselves, respecting their freedom.', 'Membership in Opus Dei requires a supernatural vocation.', '(celibate members) sometimes practice [sic] traditional Catholic penances such as using the cilice [garment of haircloth] and discipline.'

Parador luxury hotel housed in a historic building.

Pilgrim (from Latin Peregrinus, stranger) although used now to describe all pilgrims, it was used in the Middle Ages specifically for pilgrims to Santiago. Pilgrims to Rome were called in Latin romipetae (whence the Spanish words Romeo, pilgrim, and Romería, local pilgrimage), while pilgrims to Jerusalem were called palmarius, in English palmers (Sp. palmeros), from the palm leaves they carried to symbolise their pilgrimage.

Pincho / Pinchos (or Pinxo) Basque for tapa (see below).

Pueblo Calle a town or village constructed according to a plan with a dense urban centre based around a main street lined with conjoined houses. The objective of this form of urban planning was to encourage a nucleus of economic activity in the centre of the village.

Plague, the (also known as the Black Death) a pandemic of bubonic plague in Europe which reached it peak around 1350. It is believed to have killed around 25 million people, a third of Europe's population.

PP (Partido Popular) Popular (as in 'of the people') Party.

Priscillian of Avila (Spanish Prisciliano) a wealthy landowner who renounced worldly goods to live the life of an ascetic. He founded a movement which practised Gnostic rituals, vegetarianism and abstention from sex and attracted many followers in northern Spain. He was the first martyr to be put to death by a Christian emperor, Magnus Maximus in 385. (see also History of the Camino and under Astorga).

PSOE (Partido Socialista Obrero Español) Spanish Socialist Workers' Party.

Reconquista (English Reconquest) refers to the historical period which culminated in the re-establishment of Christian political domination of the Iberian Peninsula.

Roldán (French Roland, English Ronald) was a commander in the army of Charlemagne who led the rearguard of the main army in Roncesvalles when it was attacked and defeated by Basque bandits on 15 August 778. La Chanson de Roland (Song of Ronald) refers to these events, transforming them into an epic and heroic struggle against an army of many thousands of Saracens (Muslims). It is considered the oldest known example of written French. The Normans are said to have sung it at the Battle of Hastings (1066).

Rollo a stone pillar, often with ornamental carvings and topped with a crucifix or some other religious symbol, erected in the Middle Ages to mark the path to Santiago and/or to commemorate some important event.

Saint James the Great (Spanish Santiago el Mayor) was one of the twelve apostles along with his brother John. Their parents were Zebedee and Salome (a sister to Jesus' mother). He is said to have proselytised in Spain before returning to Jerusalem where he died by beheading in the year 44 at the hand of King Herod Agrippa.

Santiago (See also Saint James the Great) is a shortened version of San Yago which in turn comes from the Hebrew name Yakob (James). Two of Jesus' apostles had this name and to distinguish between them they are usually called James the Great and James the Lesser. It is the remains of James the Great that are reputed to be in Santiago de Compostela.

Scallop-shell is the symbol traditionally worn by pilgrims returning from Santiago. Its origins are unclear but it is documented in relation to Santiago from the early Middle Ages. There are various theories as to its symbolism, such as, a representation of the setting sun in Finisterre, a fertility symbol, a representation of brotherly love or symbolising legends associated with St James such as the one about the Galician prince who fell in the sea on his horse and was pulled from the waves covered in scallop-shells by St James. Whatever its origin, the scallop-shell became so popular and important that it influenced the traditional portrayal of St James introducing the elements of the pilgrim's hat and scallop-shell. The symbol has pre-Christian origins having been used in connection with the Greek goddess Aphrodite.

Segmental Arch an arch in which the curve is less than a semicircular segment of a circle.

Tapa (pl Tapas) is the generic name given to the variety of snacks served in Spanish cafés. Not all cafés serve Tapas and those that do are mostly in urban areas. There is an infinite variety of Tapas and the most common are listed in the Menu Guide.

Ultreia from the Codex Calixtinus (G) from Latin Ultre ia et sus eia! Deus adjuva nos! / Lets go further and higher! God help us!

Wellington, Duke of, aka Arthur Wellsey, aka The Iron Duke. Born of an Anglo-Irish family in County Meath, he rose to prominence during the Peninsular Wars, became Ambassador to France and commanded British forces at the Battle of Waterloo. Asked about his Irish origins, the good Duke is reputed to have said, 'Being born in a stable does not make one a horse.'

Xacobeo (Spanish Jacobeo) is the Galician adjective to describe things associated with St James. The Holy Year (G) is often referred to simply as O Xacobeo.

Placenames

SPANISH

Burgo = Hamlet/Village
Calzada = Road (calzada romana Roman road)
Campo = Field
Casa = House
Conde = Count
Franco / Franca = a place colonised by Franks or freemen (G)
Itero = Riverbank
Laguna / Lago = Lake
Mayor = Big
Menor = Little
Molina = Mill
Monte = Hill/Mountain
Plaza = Square
Puente/Pon = Bridge
Real = Royal
Río = River
San/Santo/Santa = Saint
Seco/Seca = Dry
Templarios = Templars
Torre = Tower
Valle/Val = Valley
Vega = Plain
Venta = Inn
Villa / Vila = Town

GALICIAN

Praza = Square
Rei = King
Rúa = Street
Palas = Palace
San/Santa = Saint

BASQUE

Berri = New
Iri (also Arre) = Village
Oki = Place
Zabal = Plain by a river
Zir = High ground
Zubi = Bridge

ARABIC

Arabic placenames are common in Spain, but more so in the south. They are easy to recognise because they are often preceded by the Arabic word for the, *al*. However, the pronunciation of *al* changes to mimic the following letter when it precedes *t*, *d*, *r*, *z*, *s*, *sh* or *n*.
  eg. al bint = the girl, ash shams = the sun, as samaa = the sky

Alcalá = the Fort
Guardal = River (from wadi as in Guadalquivir, Guadalhorce, Guadiana)
Valladolid = Land of Walid (Arabic Balad al-Walid)

Breathable and "waterproof" materials

Waterproof is in quotes in the title because the materials used to give modern hiking gear its waterproofing aren't strictly speaking "waterproof". Take the example of **Gore-Tex**, probably the most common waterproofing material used by pilgrims. Gore-Tex is a trade name of expanded *polytetrafluoroethylene* (PTFE). PTFE is a type of semi-permeable membrane - it allows some things to pass through it, but not others. It can do this because it has billions of tiny holes. Liquid water cannot pass through these holes, but water vapour molecules **can**. This means that rain stays out but sweat, transformed into water vapour by your body heat, can get out.
  Other materials, such as Polyurethane (PU), use similar technology.
  "Gore-Tex" rainwear actually consists of several layers of material, only one of which is PTFE. For example, Gore-Tex jackets typically have one or more hard-wearing outer layers, designed to protect the inner layers. Then a layer of PTFE and, underneath that, several other layers to give the jacket the required thermal insulation.
  The same applies to "Gore-Tex" boots. They usually have a leather outer layer, then a PTFE layer and a few other layers inside that.
  How long your rainwear remains waterproof depends on how much you use it and how well you look after it. Good quality rainwear it should come with an information leaflet on how to look after it. This will probably involve instructions on washing and using a specified product for cleaning and restoring breathability.

Pilgrim associations

The national associations, whatever they chose to call themselves, are the modern equivalent of the medieval confraternities which existed to offer advice and assistance to pilgrims. Many of them organise meeting and informative events for would-be pilgrims, issue *Credenciales*, sell guide books, train *hospitaleros*, etc.

Canada
Canadian Company of Pilgrims   *www.santiago.ca*
    ou bien, en français   *www.duquebecacompostelle.org*
Ireland
Irish Society of the Friends of St James   *www.stjamesirl.com*
South Africa
Confraternity of St James of South Africa   *www.csjofsa.za.org*
UK
Confraternity of St James   *www.csj.org.uk*
USA
American Pilgrims on the Camino   *www.americanpilgrims.com*
Australia
Australian Friends of the Camino   *www.afotc.org*
New Zealand
A page on the CSJ website is dedicated to   *www.csj.org.uk/newzealand.htm*
Kiwi pilgrims

Copyright notice

Thanks

Thanks for buying this book and I hope it has been useful to you. If you have any comments, suggestions or questions you can contact me at *info@caminoguide.net*
    Nothing remains now but to wish you **Buen Camino!**

Walking Guide to the Camino de Santiago

The author of this book has also written a practical guide to walking the Camino Francés called *Walking Guide to the Camino de Santiago, History - Culture – Architecture*.

Intended for traditional pilgrims walking the Camino and staying in pilgrim hostels, it contains clearly presented and up-to-date (as of 2014) information on accommodation and services as well as route descriptions and urban and rural maps. There's also a wealth of information about the places you'll pass through, their historical connections to pilgrimage, the architecture of their magnificent buildings, and the history of the people who live there.

Like this book, it's carefully and thoroughly researched and contains all the essential information you'll need when walking the Camino, presented in a fair and even-handed manner.

Its size and weight are almost identical to this book.

It's available in book format and in the same ebook formats as this book, and from the same websites. Just search for **Walking Guide to the Camino de Santiago**, or link directly to it from *www.CaminoGuide.net*.

RURAL MAPS

Showing the route of the Camino, towns and villages and the facilities you'll find there.

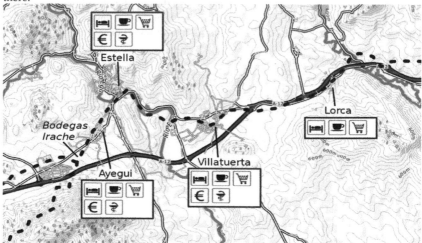

URBAN MAPS

There are street maps of all the main towns and villages showing the location of hostels and other sights of interest.

Since it is intended for pilgrims who wish to stay in pilgrim hostels, it does not contain information about hotels or guesthouses. If you want to stay exclusively in private accommodate you would be better off considering one of the other guides such as Mr Brierley's *Pilgrim's Guide to the Camino de Santiago*, which is widely available from bookshops or online, or the Confraternity of St James, *Camino Francés* guide, which is available from their website *www.csj.org.uk*. However, please also note that hotels and guesthouses advertise extensively along the Camino and that Tourist Information Offices give out free lists with information on all types of accommodation, which would serve your needs fine if you wanted to occasionally have the option for a bit of privacy.